scending to
Glory

The Secret of

Personal Prayer

by

Dr. Judson Cornwall

Fire Wind™

Mansfield, PA

Fire Wind, an imprint of
Kingdom Publishing
P.O. Box 506
Mansfield, PA 16933
(570) 662-7515
(800) 597-1123

This book was formerly titled *The Secret of Personal Prayer* before the update and revision.

First printing, July 1988; Second printing, September 1988; Third printing, May 1989; Fourth printing, February 1991; Fifth printing, March 1999

 *scending to Glory*

Preface 5

1 Prayer Is a Divine Provision 9

2 Prayer Ascends As the Channel for Confession 25

3 Prayer Ascends As the Channel for Petition 39

4 Prayer Ascends As the Channel for
        Communication 55

5 Prayer Ascends As the Channel for Intercession 71

6 Prayer Ascends As the Channel for the Release
        of Faith 87

7 Prayer Ascends As the Channel for Submission 101

8 Prayer Ascends As the Channel for
        Thanksgiving 117

9 Prayer Ascends As the Channel for Praise 133

10 Prayer Ascends As the Channel for Adoration 147

Notes 157

Acknowledgment

My wife, Eleanor, has taken great pride in the writing of this book. Thank you, dear, for your support. Only another writer can understand what this support means.

My thanks go to my secretary, Terri Gargis. Her help in research and her faithful and often painful hours at the computer have not gone unnoticed by me or by God.

Dedication

To Charles and Estelle DeFelippo who have long stood with me as partners in this ministry. Their prayers have repeatedly touched the throne of God for me. The apostle Paul had to request the prayers of the saints for his ministry. The two of you volunteered to pray for me. Only heaven will reveal the results.

 *reface*

Prayer should never be viewed merely as an emergency procedure. It should be the normal, day-by-day communion between a believer and the Almighty God. He has promised, "Call to me, and I will answer you, and show you great and mighty things, which you do not know" (Jeremiah 33:3).

Whenever there is a new emphasis on prayer in the church, a fresh release of power comes upon the congregation. As a pastor, I discovered that prayer became the root structure of the tree God was growing among the people I served. Every growth upward had to be balanced with an increase of the root structure downward. As we grew numerically, we increased our prayer schedule. I had been raised to believe: "Much prayer; much power. Little prayer; little power. No prayer; no power!" To this day, I cannot see this as a simple motto. It is an enduring truth that continues to be as valid as John 3:16.

What is true of a collective body of believers is equally true of individual Christians. To remain prayerless is to live without a vital contact with God. Prayer ascends to glory as the communication channel from our spirit to the Spirit of God. Prayer is our cell phone! Prayer allows us to rise into God's presence and discuss whatever is important to us at the moment.

Prayer does not pull God down to our level; prayer allows us to move upward to God's level. In the language of David, communion with God enables us to "ascend into the hill of the Lord" (Psalms 24:3). It lets us escape from our time-space dimension and enter briefly into eternity.

Jacob, running from the wrath of his brother, spent a night in the barren wilderness. There he had an unexpected encounter with God. "Then he dreamed, and behold, a ladder was set up on the earth, and its top reached to heaven; and there the angels of God were ascending and descending on it" (Genesis 28:12). Jacob was greatly comforted in the knowledge that . God's messenger went upward to God before heaven's communication came downward to man. Jesus referred to Jacob's encounter when he spoke to His disciple, Phillip: "He said to him, 'Most assuredly, I say to you, hereafter you shall see heaven open, and the angels of God ascending and descending upon the Son of man" (John 1:51). Here Jesus defines Himself as that ladder Jacob saw. In God's glorious plan, communication goes up to heaven and back down to earth upon Jesus. He burned a hole through Satan's kingdom in the sky—making access to God as simple as getting to Jesus.

In the final book of the Bible, John saw a golden altar with burning incense, "And the smoke of the incense, with the prayers of the saints, ascended before God from the angel's hand" (Revelation 8:4). Prayer may begin in the corner of a basement or from the seclusion of a prison cell, but it ascends higher and higher until it reaches the very face of God. When our prayers reach heaven, an angel of God mixes heaven's incense of prayer with our earthly prayer: When the cloud of incense ascends to the throne of God, it carries the right fragrance.

There is still another way we can view prayer as ascending. Prayer is communication, and all communication is a learned art. Just as we don't learn to speak in one quick lesson, we don't learn to pray effectively in one prayer meeting. Our praying usually starts from a very selfish level and slowly rises to an unselfish level of communicating love to God. We often begin praying in fear and desperation. Regularly spending time in the presence of God transforms our desperate cries into prayers of faith and delight in His glorious sovereignty.

In this book, I examine nine different levels of prayer; from confession—the first channel of communion, to adoration—the height of prayer. Each level ascends higher into glory than the preceding levels. As a preteen preacher, most of my prayer was centered on confession and petition, but as I matured and my concepts of God enlarged, so did my method of prayer. I never completely forsook earlier forms of prayer; I grew from them as a tree grows out of its root structure. My purpose is not to downgrade any form of prayer. The lowest level of prayer is an improvement over prayerlessness. I simply want to share what I have discovered and experienced over the years.

There are glorious excursions in prayer that can be exciting and enriching to the person who dares to take the higher path once in a while. Just as the husband and wife who always say the same things to each other will soon lose interest in talking to each other, the praying person who fails to enlarge his or her forms of communication with God will eventually lose interest in praying.

It is my earnest hope that this book will act as a guide to those who desire to leave the valleys of prayer and climb to the mountains of blessing, where communicating with God eventually draws all attention away from oneself and focuses all thought and expressions upon God Himself.

Judson Cornwall
Phoenix, AZ

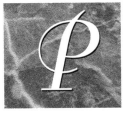 rayer is a Divine Provision

Brilliant King Solomon wrote, "He [God] has made everything beautiful in its time. Also He has put eternity in their hearts" (Ecclesiastes 3:11*a*). Solomon must have been divinely inspired to couple earthly beauty with an inner awareness of eternity. When one looks at the ceaseless movement of the majestic ocean or stands at the rim of the Grand Canyon and peers into its awesome depths and rugged beauty, it is almost impossible to ignore the inner awareness of something higher than nature. However it may be defined, there seems to be an involuntary reaching out to eternity when we look thoughtfully at the beauty of our world.

Though this innate knowledge is both self-evident and ever-present, it cannot be demonstrated in a test tube or stored in a computer. Consequently, many try to deny its existence, but what is known in the heart cannot be countermanded by the mind. Even avowed atheists have been heard to exclaim, "I thank God that I'm an atheist" which, of course, is a grave contradiction. The first statement is an expression of the heart, while the second is an attempt to overrule that heart knowledge with the rationalization of the mind. The heart knows what the mind cannot yet comprehend: there is, indeed, something or Someone higher.

The Bible teaches us that prayer is the glorious channel God has provided for mortal humans to ascend into these eternal realms of God's dwelling. In great anguish David testified, "The Lord has heard my supplication; the Lord will receive my prayer" (Psalms 6:9). God's provision works! From Genesis to Revelation we see men and women using the prayer channel to communicate with God and to allow God to communicate with them. The testimony that David's son Solomon gave to the world is "The Lord...hears the prayer of the righteous" (Proverbs 15:29).

All the writers of the New Testament extol prayer as a vibrant part of a believer's contact with God. The four Gospel writers portray Jesus as a praying man, and they record His teachings on prayer. Paul also was a great exponent of prayer, writing, "I desire therefore that the men pray everywhere, lifting up holy hands, without wrath and doubting" (1 Timothy 2:8). The writer of the book of Hebrews pled, "Pray for us" (Hebrews 13:18a), while the apostle James wrote, "The effective, fervent prayer of a righteous man avails much" (James 5:16b). Peter, "the rock," quoted the psalmist who said, "For the eyes of the Lord are on the righteous, and His ears are open to their prayers" (1 Peter 3:12a).

John, the beloved, went even further by saying, "Now this is the confidence that we have in Him, that if we ask anything according to His will, He hears us. And if we know that He hears us, whatever we ask, we know that we have the petitions that we have asked of Him" (1 John 5:14,15). Even Jude, in his very brief book, exhorted us, "But you, beloved, building yourselves up on your most holy faith, praying in the Holy Spirit, keep yourselves in the love of God" (Jude 20,21a). Obviously, prayer was important to the eight or more writers of the New Testament.

Furthermore, all of the holy men and women of history were persons of prayer. They were aware that prayer bridged the gulf between time and eternity, and they acted on that awareness by praying until they touched the heart of God. It was not their knowledge, but their acting on that knowledge, that made them such threats to kings on earth and to spiritual principalities in the heavens.

Prayer as a Commodity

In our generation, prayer seems to be less an action and more a commodity that can be manufactured, marketed, and microwaved to be served as needed. It is packaged in a great variety of ways, and it is presented to people much as groceries are sold. We have prayer chains, prayer calendars, prayer days, and nights of prayer. We take turns praying; we send money for others to pray for us; we even have "dial-a-prayer" in many communities. In our churches, we seem to specialize in "a word" of prayer, or we unite to recite a prayer dictated by the pastor. We are not unaware of prayer, *but we seem to be unable actually to pray.*

Edith really loved the Lord and believed that He would intervene in personal affairs. Though she faithfully handed in her prayer requests to the intercessory prayer group, Edith was not confident that she could contact God herself personally. So, on Thursday nights when prayer requests were often accepted in the service, we could count on her to have one or more petitions for us to pray over.

My sister, who was my associate pastor at the time, accepted Edith as a challenge. She taught her to pray—not just for needs—but for fellowship with God. Though Edith was confined to her home with three small children and no transportation, she learned to contact God right where she was. As Edith's prayer time became more and more vital in her relationship with God, her requests for our prayers diminished rapidly. Before long, she was phoning the church asking if there were any requests she could take as a prayer burden. To this day she lifts my sister and I in prayer as she fellowships with God. She successfully moved from seeing prayer as a commodity to being in communion with the Living God.

Has there ever been a time when Americans were more conscious of prayer than at the present time? Television has repeatedly shown us thousands of Moslems prostrated on their prayer rugs, their heads face toward Mecca in one of their three daily ritual prayer sessions. Recent news reports have pictured zealous Tibetans pushing their way through crowds of worshippers, seeking to touch the golden shaft of a prayer wheel; prayers written and attached to these wind-operated prayer wheels are viewed as magic charms. Each turn of the wheel signifies the repetition of that prayer which some god somewhere, somehow, is to read and respond to favorably.

On other occasions, television has flashed footage of crowds of American protesters forming a "prayer vigil" in hopes of preventing an execution or the construction of a nuclear power station. Lighted candles and protest songs are presented as prayers. If what the visual news media show is all there is to prayer, then prayer is a religious ritual, a magic amulet or a form of civil protest; but no truly born-again Christian could accept this definition of prayer, even though subconsciously one or all of these concepts underlie much Christian prayer.

From time to time, the churches in America join together to have a prayer congress, a prayer watch, or a prayer retreat; but these often end up being preaching conferences rather than prayer sessions. Often what is projected as prayer is an attempt to control God through various forms of vocal commands issued to the Almighty. Some of these utterances have been very learned and presented by seasoned orators; other presentations have been extremely fervent and emotional. But, either way, were they prayers as the Bible defines prayer?

Earnest Christians are conscious of the need for prayer, but one wonders if they really understand the nature of prayer; for—in spite of this awareness—few Christians pray regularly. We know that we are to pray, but we do not pray. We view prayer as a divine law, but we live in disobedience to that law, except in dire emergencies. We are much like the wealthy widow on an ocean liner enroute from England to America. When a severe Atlantic storm hit the ship, she used her influence to gain admission to the bridge. There she demanded that the captain "do something."

"Everything that can be done has been done," he replied. "We are in the hands of God now; we can only pray."

Hearing this, the woman cried, "Captain, has it come to that?" and then she fainted in fear.

Prayer should not be a last resort; it should be our initial reaction. We are not appealing to heaven's Supreme Court; we are talking to our heavenly Father. Prayer is far more communing with a Person than it is conforming to a law. It is not so much getting things from God; it is getting to God. Nor is prayer a commanding of God; it is communion with God.

I saw that in a man named Howard. Quietly he slipped into the congregation. If it hadn't been for my head usher's report, I would never have known that he had visited. The church I pastored was in the middle of a building program. Howard showed up for a work night and volunteered to help us. This man was what we desperately needed—a plumber. Working with him, I found him to be a man of quiet peace. He gave off the air that everything was perfect in his life. It wasn't until we had worked together for several weeks that I found out he was a pastor who had been deeply wounded by his former congregation and had entered the work force for a time of inner healing.

As I got to know Howard, he showed himself to be a man of quiet prayer and great confidence in the grace of God. He preferred not to be called on for public prayer, but at times it seemed that every breath he breathed was a quiet prayer to God. It didn't surprise me that, when the building was complete, he was given a call to pastor a church in a neighboring state and went on to the strongest ministry of his career.

I find that one of the quickest ways to elicit guilt in a congregation of believers is to talk about a prayer life. Even though

> Prayer should not be a last resort; it should be our initial reaction.

the motivation is not to project guilt, and even though the message is not a legalistic approach to a prayer life, the very mention of prayer brings guilt to the minds of most believers. While they give lip service to prayer, they do not give live action to prayer.

Perhaps we are too involved with this natural world to be willing to invest time in the spiritual world through prayer. We are responding to the insistent demands of life, while ignoring the instinctive desires of our spirits.

Our eyes are so riveted upon earthly things that we are blind to spiritual realities, and the call of "things" drowns out the call of God's Spirit. While prayer seems to be profitable, it has a very low place on our priority list. Little wonder that we have lost our inner peace and the sense of the presence of God.

Prayerless Christians are somewhat like the lost hiker trying desperately to survive his thirst in the heat of the desert sun. Sitting in the shade of a large saguaro cactus, he doesn't realize that the very cactus that affords him shade is filled with water that could save his life. He would only have to cut into its storage reserve. Prayer allows us to reach into the hidden resources of God Himself and draw out the needed supply of life. But for that to become a reality, prayer must become more than a marketable commodity. True prayer starts as a Commitment.

Prayer as a Commitment

There is a very real sense in which prayer has its beginnings in God Himself. No matter how deep a heart's longing may be, none would attempt to make contact with God unless some outside provision is made for an audience with Him. In speaking of our Lord Jesus Christ, Paul said, "...He who is the blessed and only Potentate, the King of kings and Lord of lords, who alone has immortality, dwelling in unapproachable light, whom no man has seen or can see, to whom be honor and everlasting power. Amen" (1 Timothy 6:15,16). No one casually drops in on such a One.

Residents of London often see large crowds of tourists standing outside Buckingham Palace looking longingly through the fence. It is likely that each person desires a chance to talk with the queen, but only those who have been extended an invitation can enter the palace, much less have an audience with her. Similarly, unless the King of kings invites us into His presence, we will not have access to Him. But He *has* invited us in! He declared, "Pray to Me, and I will listen to you" (Jeremiah 29:12*b*). In the oldest book of the Bible, Elihu, one of Job's comforters, said, "He shall pray to God, and He will delight in him; he shall see His face with joy, for He restores to man His righteousness" (Job 33:26). This is God's invitation into His presence. The person who will pray is promised a hearing, and God promises to delight in that person. Then God offers to give divine righteousness to the praying individual.

Sometimes I have watched TV evangelists get "earnest" in their praying. They parade from one side of the platform to the other—screaming into the mike, waving their arms, and even stomping their feet. It appears they feel that their volume and physical gestures insure their prayers getting through. It does remind one of the prophets of Baal who acted similarly to awaken their god. It isn't fervency that gets our prayers through to God, it is faith in His provision. He is not so far off to be yelled at; He lives in the hearts of believers. He need not be coerced—just communicated with. Why do we make prayer so complicated, when God made it so simple?

14

Prayer, then, is not overcoming God's reluctance; it is responding to God's provision. It is not forcing our way into God's presence like a

Prayer is more than a polite interview with God...

gate-crasher at a party; God has already granted us an audience. Prayer is merely taking advantage of that invitation. The appointment has been made; it is up to us to keep it. God has committed Himself to be available to the person who will pray; and in that availability, He has promised to listen and to respond. Jesus promised, "Whatever you ask in My name, that will I do, that the Father may be glorified in the Son" (John 14:13).

Prayer is more than a polite interview with God at which we have our picture taken with Him so we can prove to our posterity that we once had an audience with Him. Prayer is a powerful interaction with God. We speak, and He listens. We ask, and He answers. It is less a beggar asking alms of the wealthy and more an ambassador reporting to his superior officer on the state of affairs in a far-off country. The initial appointment of ambassadorship carries with it the right and the responsibility to communicate with the one who assigned him to that country. Paul told us, "We are ambassadors for Christ" (2 Corinthians 5:20a). This assures us the right of access to the living God.

But prayer is far more than God's commitment to grant us access to Himself and to give us a joyful hearing. Prayer is equally a commitment made by persons to God. Prayer is not automatic. It demands discipline, dedication, and determination; for prayer requires us to contact the spiritual realm in which God dwells. This involves far more effort than merely picking up the phone to call a close friend across the nation. God said, "You will seek Me and find Me, when you search for Me with all your heart" (Jeremiah 29:13). Prayer involves a seeking and a searching, and this calls for a commitment to continue this search until we find God; then we will have a prayer audience with Him.

Twenty or more years ago, I was deeply impressed by the walk with God a friend of mine demonstrated. When I told him that I would give anything to have the relationship he had with God, he said, "I don't think that you are a strong enough person to do what it takes to have an intimate relationship with God."

This, of course, challenged me; and I insisted that I was far stronger than he knew.

Smiling, he said, "Judson, to have fellowship with God, you would have to discipline yourself to spend much time every day in prayer, and—with your present church involvements—I don't think you would be able to do it."

I told him that I had been a person of prayer for many years, but he persisted, "I don't mean praying for the needs of your congregation or for God to give you a sermon for Sunday. I mean fellowshipping with God in the communion of prayer until you get to know His heart and will."

I realized that he was prodding me to make a commitment, and I did so. First, I committed an hour, then two; and, after I had become comfortable with that, I added a third hour of daily prayer. It was the beginning of a gradual, but dynamic, change in me and in my relationship with God. I came to love those times in His divine presence—and I still do—but I had to learn continually to honor my daily commitment to pray, because constant pressures for involvement tried to push into the slot of time I had set aside for time with Him.

Prayer, for me, starts with the disciplined honoring of a commitment I have made to God. Christians who pray only when "the Spirit moves them" seldom develop depth in their relationship with God, for they require divine prodding or enticement to approach God. They fail to exercise the option to pray that God has extended to them, completely ignoring the truth that prayer commitment is two-sided. God's commitment to us requires a commitment from us to God. He has made Himself available to us; now we must make ourselves available to Him, if prayer is to be the interaction God has purposed it to be. Communication always requires at least two persons. But prayer is not merely a commitment. It is a command.

Prayer as a Command

The democratic principle that underlies America's government has given us a marvelous sense of the worth of the individual, but it has also tended to weaken the force of authority. Personal opinion and individual desire are regularly weighed against law, and this attitude follows us into the church. The Bible is no longer the rule of authority in the lives of thousands of Christians; and, while Jesus is embraced as Savior, He is not acknowledged as Lord. These persons approach the Bible as though it were a book of suggestions from which they could choose a quaint saying or a useful maxim to use as a guideline for the day while ignoring the clear commands of God's Word. Just as the motorist who has been pulled to the side of the road by a state trooper will learn from the issued ticket that personal opinion does not establish the speed limit, so Christians often learn very painfully that their concepts do not alter God's commands. As Corrie ten Boom reminded us years ago, "The Bible contains no suggestions; only commandments."

One of the clear, concise commandments written repeatedly in God's Word is "Pray!" That word occurs over 250 times in our Bible, while "prayer," "prayers" and "praying" appear an additional 280 times. We are far more than invited to pray; we are commanded repeatedly to pray—even by the Lord Jesus Christ Himself, who said, "Take heed, and pray" (Mark 13:33a). Prayerlessness, then, is personal disobedience: A clear command has been countermanded.

Commands can induce either resistance or response, depending on the attitude of our hearts. David declared, "I delight to do Your will, O my God, and Your law is within my heart" (Psalm 40:8), and the author of Hebrews quotes Jesus as saying, "Behold, I have come to do Your will, O God" (Hebrews 10:9a). David and Jesus delighted in the expressed will of God the Father because they had learned the superiority of the will. God does not command us to pray as a form of chastisement or discipline. Prayer is as necessary to spiritual life as scuba tanks are to the physical life of a deep-sea diver. Prayer is the atmosphere in which a human spirit can function comfortably. It is the breath of eternity so necessary to our eternal spirits that are confined in temporal bodies. When prayer is cut off, a human spirit smothers; when God commands us to "watch and pray" (Matthew 26:41*a*), He's saying, "Breathe deeply."

But, you may ask, why do we need to be commanded to breathe?

Perhaps our natural life is somewhat like the womb experience: Everything the unborn child needs is supplied through the umbilical cord. Upon birth, however, this cord is severed and the baby must breathe or perish. The slap of the doctor on the inverted infant induces a reflex action that causes the baby to start breathing. It is the radical change of environment that makes breathing necessary for the baby.

Similarly, when our soul-spirit is brought into the realm of God, we experience a radical change that demands deep spiritual breathing. We are no longer supplied from an umbilical cord attached to the natural world. Paul put it: "Therefore, if anyone is in Christ, he is a new creation; old things have passed away; behold, all things have become new" (2 Corinthians 5:17).

Prayer patterns differ with individuals. Some people take three or four days each quarter to retreat from life to seek God; others reserve half a day each week for prayer. If this is supplementary to daily prayer, I can see its value. If, however, this is the extent of their prayer lives, I wonder how they can survive from quarter to quarter or even week to week without breathing. My human lungs do not want a great expanse of air on a monthly basis; they require a gentle filling several times each minute. Does not our spiritual nature require a consistent supply of the breath of God?

Prayer as a Challenge

While prayer is commanded explicitly in the Scriptures, it is also projected mercifully as a challenge. God issued such a challenge through the prophet Jeremiah: "Call to Me, and I will answer you, and show you great and mighty things, which you do not know" (Jeremiah 33:3). First, God puts the ball in our court with the challenge "Call to Me!" Then He volleys with "I will answer you," and He follows through with "[I will] show you great and mighty things, which you do not know."

If we do not get involved with Him in prayer, we will miss His answers and His revelations. The things we wish God would write in the sky, He has chosen to write in our hearts—through prayer. No communication with God; no revelation from God. The challenge is real, but it is equally realistic. God never commands us to do the impossible or the unreasonable. He first gives us the prayer channel, and then He challenges us to use it for our own benefit. He commands us to pray, but He also explains the personal advantages to prayer. What a challenge! Communication and revelation are offered as by-products of prayer.

From my boyhood days on, I had no goal in life other than to be a pastor. I chose my high school and college courses with this in mind, and I moved from an assistant pastor in a large church to a senior pastor of a small church when I was still in my late teens. Being a pastor of a growing congregation completely fulfilled my life.

Then calls began to come from other congregations asking me to share with them the truths that had become so dynamic in my congregation. Out of these calls came invitations to share in conferences and conventions, and ministry in other countries opened up. This sent me to prayer. Although I tried it for about three years, I eventually realized that I could not continue to pastor and be a traveling man.

The more I prayed, the more convinced I became that God wanted to make a major change in my portfolio of ministry. He was pushing me into a traveling ministry with writing as a side ministry. I found it extremely threatening. I enjoyed the security of a weekly check and a loving congregation. I had just built a new home for my wife and family, and I did not want to leave it.

The unknown factors in the ministry that lay before me were intimidating. I understood God's leading not as a sugges-tion but as a command. A loving command—yes, but still a command; and although I had no desire to rebel, I lacked a strong impulse to obey. The more I spent time in the presence of God in my prayer chamber, the greater my awareness became of His promise to go with me everywhere I would go. That assurance was enough to cause me to sever the lines to my pastoring ministry and make myself available to the wider

19

body of Christ. God's calling cut across all my longing for security and all my preconceived notions of what I was to do with my life.

But God is not the only force in the universe that challenges believers to pray. Life itself hurls the challenge: "Change me." Many persons have been bitterly disappointed to discover that conversion did not change the circumstances of their lives, rather it changed their relationships to God. If they were experiencing the pain of divorce when they embraced Jesus Christ as their Lord, they still felt the pain after their salvation; their conversions did not throw the divorces out of court, even though they had gained the peaceful presence of the Lord dwelling within them. The emptiness and loneliness of a new life-style became a challenge to change. Those who accepted God's offered help, and gave themselves to prayer, found the spiritual power and divine wisdom they needed to go on and make a new life for themselves. Others lived in anger and self-pity until life atrophied, leaving them bitter shells of what they had once been.

Praying Christians can find their way through a great variety of life's reverses. They have access to God, who has faithfully promised them His grace, guidance, and

> Prayer is the channel through which God gets involved in our everyday affairs.

strength, though not automatically. These helps come to those who ask for them. Prayer is the channel through which God gets involved in our everyday affairs. No prayer; no intervention.

It seems that we have arrived at a juncture in church history when the local church is challenging its individual members to give themselves to prayer. We've been in a protracted season where programs have dominated the church. We've built great buildings, enjoyed numerical growth, and established work-able structures; but, people are asking, "Where is Jesus?" Trained workers on church staffs want to know, "When will we do the things that Jesus did?"

The congregations that are accepting this as a challenge to pray are experiencing both the power and the presence of the

Lord when they gather to worship. God is always more eager to manifest Himself among us than we are to have His presence, but the initial contact is ours—through prayer.

Most church situations that we attempt to control through ballots and business meetings could more rapidly and less painfully be handled through fervent prayer. After all, it is God's church, isn't it? If we would call, He would answer and show us the solution. Perhaps more church supper rooms should be converted to *upper rooms* where we intercede with God, rather than socialize politically with the saints. Our desperate need for the mind of Christ can be met only through consistent, faith-filled praying. This is not a new need, but it is a new challenge to this generation.

Prayer as a Catharsis

When Peter wrote, "casting all your care upon Him, for He cares for you" (1 Peter 5:7), he offered believers a channel for the removal of negative emotions, such as anxiety, fear and anger. Prayer is a catharsis for the soul-spirit; it releases the overload that our highly-industrialized life has forced upon us. Prayer casts that load upon the Lord. It transfers the weight of life from the weak to the strong.

This principle of release has been adapted by our secular society. I have read several articles by practicing psychologists who urge people to have a daily quiet time during which they vocalize their frustrations and anxieties. Some writers have even dared to call it "prayer," while emphasizing that it is not necessary to believe in God to benefit from prayer. It hurts me to see businessmen dedicating up to an hour a day to the catharsis of prayer without knowing that there is a God with whom they could be enjoying fellowship during that time. They are merely unloading their crowded psyches. On the other hand, Christians are emptying their cares and enjoying the presence of the One "who cares for you."

The popularity of transcendental meditation with its assigned prayer mantra finds its roots in this same law of life: Prayer unlocks our inner nature. The meditative repetition of the secret word—the mantra—flushes the emotional nature much as a physic purges the digestive system. Satan, who got all of his spiritual on-the-job training in heaven, knows—better than the saints on earth—how powerful prayer can be; so he has coined a substitute that meets some of the needs of our inner nature without allowing us to contact God.

Although the cathartic value of prayer is among the lowest reasons for praying, it is very real. Life is full of uncertainty and stress—even for devout believers. Decision follows decision, and need piles upon need. We feel as if we are on a treadmill that seems to run faster every year. Most of us have to run just to keep our place in life. Like a twenty-amp circuit breaker that is being forced to carry an ever-increasing overload, we are about to trip and break the circuit of life. We just can't handle it anymore.

When I pastored, I carried a heavy counseling load. At the end of a day, I would often be exhausted emotionally,

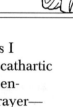

Our overload protection is prayer.

weighted down with the needs of my congregation. As I entered into a life of prayer, I discovered that it had a cathartic value. I learned to schedule my counseling with a fifteen-minute break between sessions. I used this time for prayer— unloading the burdens and pressures I had picked up in the previous session. This left me fresh and unburdened to face the next person. After all, God is the burden bearer, isn't He? But He can bear only what we entrust into His care through personal prayer.

Every year we see more and more believers, and even full-time Christian workers, listed among the suicide victims. Their faith did not prevent a serious overload, and something vital exploded in them. They just couldn't cope with the overload that life had forced upon them.

But God has made provision for a relieving safety valve. That overload protection is prayer. Instead of allowing pressure to build day after day, we should cast all our cares upon Him, for He cares for us. We need to unload on a daily basis and cut down on the build-up of tension, anxiety, fear, frustration and hatred. As we take them to God in prayer, He will listen patiently, share the burdens paternally, and counsel us particularly. We will be received, relieved, and redirected by God.

The current catch-phrase among full-time Christian workers is "burnout." The heavy schedule many of them keep and the constant pressure of people and their problems take a toll on the emotions and physical energies of men and women of God. If their expended energies are not replenished regularly, exhaustion sets in, and they claim burnout.

Like the person who has inhaled the fumes of a dangerous chemical, we need to expel the bad air and inhale the good. When we come before God in prayer to breathe out the poisons our spirit-soul has inhaled, we need to learn also to take a deep breath of the presence of God. "Bad air out; good air in" should be the attitude of praying persons, for God has promised, "Those who wait on the Lord shall renew their strength; they shall mount up with wings like eagles, they shall run and not be weary, they shall walk and not faint" (Isaiah 40:31).

Earlier this year, I sat in the front room of a fifth floor walk-up apartment in Berlin. My host was a former psychiatrist who had given himself to the work of the Lord after his conversion. He pastors a congregation of 2,000 people who worship in a rented warehouse in West Berlin. Having just told me about the staff of workers he heads, the Bible school he leads, and the daily radio broadcast he airs, he shared with me his plans to begin a weekly television program—which is a real pioneer action for Europe.

"Dear brother," I said, "please accept a word of caution from an older minister. You have only so much energy. If you spread yourself too thin, you will not have sufficient strength to continue. In addition to your expanding ministry, you have a wife and five children who need you."

"I understand what you are saying," he responded. "I now pray three hours daily. If I do, indeed, go on TV, I have promised God that I will increase that to four hours of daily prayer."

"Please ignore what I just said," I replied. "With that prayer schedule, you'll make it." He had obviously learned the secret of unloading his tensions upon God in prayer and receiving divine strength in return. Prayer has become a cathartic and a motivating strength for him, and so it must be for us.

Prayer as Ascending Communication

Prayer is a marvelous, divine provision without which we could not long survive. But prayer is far more a channel than it is a commodity. God has provided this channel of communication with Himself to meet a variety of our human needs. Just as no one food will consistently meet the needs of the human body, so no one form of prayer will constantly meet the needs of the soul-spirit within us. God has provided ascending levels of communication that meet higher and higher needs in our lives. These levels bring us into greater degrees of the presence of God and give us fuller revelations of His nature. No one level of prayer can bring us into a complete fellowship with God. In any prayer session, we may move through eight or nine different levels of prayer, always ascending higher and higher into the glorious revelation of God.

Since our response to God will always be limited by our concepts of God, higher responses demand greater concepts. God is a self-revealing God. He proceeds from the known to the unknown, but He is never content to allow us to live too long at any level of revelation. He yearns to have us know Him in His fullness, so we can respond more fully to Him.

For Reflection

1. In what way may prayer have become a "commodity" in your life?
2. Do you see a commitment to pray as a burden or a blessing?
3. Do you respond to God's command to pray with gladness or with guilt?
4. Does your prayer commune with God, or do you just "talk"?

rayer Ascends As the Channel for Confession

The English language changes constantly. Some words are added; others are deleted; the meaning of still others is changed through day-to-day usage. Here in America, television has made a great impact upon our language. It has not increased our vocabularies as much as it has limited our concept of the meaning of a word to a single definition.

A good example of this is the word *confession*. The myriad of detective and police stories that flood the airwaves have virtually reduced the meaning of confession to the admission of guilt. "I confess" is the punch line for many of these shows. While this is an accurate use of the word, we need not limit the word to that concept, for confess also means "to embrace" or "to acknowledge." It is a positive, rather than negative, action. It accepts rather than admits.

This is the way the translators use the word in Paul's statement: "Therefore God also has highly exalted Him [Jesus] and given Him the name which is above every name, that at the name of Jesus every knee should bow, of those in heaven, and of those on earth, and of those under the earth, and that every tongue should *confess* that Jesus Christ is Lord, to the glory of God the Father" (Philippians 2:9-11, italics added). God's exaltation of Jesus is intended to cause all people to acknowledge—confess—the divinity of Christ.

Confession for Conversion

The process whereby a sinner elects to become a saint is called conversion—a 180-degree change in direction in life. It is also called *the new birth* or being *born again* and being *in Christ*. From God's side, this is a very complex operation involving law, guilt, punishment, and pardon. From a human point of view, however, it is really quite simple—believing, confessing, and receiving. Unfortunately, religion tends to reverse this by making human action complex while oversimplifying the work of Christ Jesus.

Salvation by works is the heart of most religious instruction, but the Bible teaches us clearly, "By grace you have been saved through faith, and that not of yourselves; it is the gift of God, not of works, lest anyone should boast" (Ephesians 2:8,9). Grace plus nothing is God's provision for salvation. There is absolutely nothing that a person can do to save himself, for it has all been done for him, or her, in Christ Jesus. God does not help us to be saved; "God is the God of salvation" (Psalms 68:20). He proposed, planned, and purchased our redemption.

God's love was demonstrated in Christ's birth: "God so loved the world that He gave His only begotten Son, that whoever believes in Him should not perish but have everlasting life" (John 3:16). God's law was answered in Christ's death: "Having now been justified by His blood, we shall be saved from wrath through Him" (Romans 5:9). And God's life was shared with persons in the resurrection of Christ Jesus from the dead, for Jesus said, "Because I live, you will live also" (John 14:19).

God's great grace offers the provision of salvation to everyone, but this does not mean, of course, that all persons are saved. This would violate the free

> Effective prayer must flow from a relationship with God, and all relationship with Him must start at Calvary.

moral agency of mankind. God's salvation has been made available to all, but it must be accepted individually before it goes into force. God's Word spells out the divine proposal very much like the offer of insurance that comes through the mail. Neither that insurance nor God's salvation goes into force until it is accepted by the individual. The signature of the applicant is a confession of acceptance of the terms stated in the insurance policy, and the "sinner's prayer" is a confession of acceptance of God's salvation.

It probably goes without argument that this must be the

beginning level of prayer. Effective prayer must flow from a relationship with God, and all relationship with Him must start at Calvary. The sin question must be settled, for God declared, "Your iniquities have separated you from your God; and your sins have hidden His face from you, so that He will not hear" (Isaiah 59:2). When the religious leaders of Christ's day summoned the man born blind to explain how Jesus could have healed him, the man answered, "Now we know that God does not hear sinners; but if anyone is a worshipper of God and does His will, He hears him" (John 9:31).

The unconverted may pray, though they have no assurance that God will listen to them, much less respond to them; but there is one prayer that God has covenanted with persons to hear and immediately respond to: "God, be merciful to me a sinner!" (Luke 18:13*b*). No one has ever prayed this in faith and been denied, for God is far more eager to save persons than they are to be saved. Peter, who had experienced much loving forgiveness by Christ after the resurrection, wrote: "The Lord is not slack concerning His promise, as some count slackness, but is longsuffering toward us, not willing that any should perish but that all should come to repentance" (2 Peter 3:9). The request for pardon is granted automatically: "Case dismissed!" is heaven's final word.

Several times I have used the services of a highly skilled person in the building trades who attends church faithfully. He has heard me in conferences and has read most, if not all, of my books. I know that he is a tither, that he reads the Bible regularly, and has times of earnest prayer. I was surprised one day to hear him say that he was looking forward to being converted. When I quizzed him about this statement, I discovered that the teaching he had received under his pastor had convinced him that he wouldn't be saved until he had experienced a dynamic conversion similar to Paul's or to some of the saints of church history. The true course of conversion— merely to believe that Christ is who He declares Himself to be, to believe that God raised Him from the dead, and then to confess this to God in the channel of prayer—seemed too simple to this friend of mine.

Unfortunately, he is not alone in this expectation of some

great spiritual experience. Salvation is far more dynamic and powerful than any of us can express in words, but our entrance into it is the simple confession of Jesus Christ as our Savior. Jesus said, "Therefore whoever confesses Me before men, him I will also confess before My Father who is in heaven" (Matthew 10:32), and "Also I say to you, whoever confesses Me before men, him the Son of Man also will confess before the angels of God" (Luke 12:8).

The key to conversion is confession. We confess Christ, and He confesses us. We do it on earth; He does it in heaven. Generally our initial confession of Christ is made directly to Christ Himself in the channel of prayer. Just as my wife-to-be wanted me to express directly to her my desire for her to marry me before I announced it to anyone else, so God invites us to confess privately His lordship over our lives before making a public declaration of that fact. First, we seal it with God in prayer; then we say it to other people as a testimony.

I am confident that I shall not live long enough to comprehend fully the power that is released in this simple prayer of confession. I have seen radical changes in lives as a result of the sinner's prayer. Confessing the lordship of Jesus means embracing His authoritative role over one's own life, and this often has both immediate and progressive effects in the behavior of persons. I have seen drunken men sober up almost instantly after praying this prayer, and I have watched broken homes reunite. I have rejoiced to see ruined lives brought back to functional productivity in society. I have seen morbid, despondent persons transformed into happy, joy-filled persons all because of the simple confession of Jesus Christ as their own Lord and Savior.

> We are transformed into the Christian life by the saving grace of a benevolent God.

How we need to remind ourselves that we are not educated into the Christian life; we are transformed into it by the saving grace of a benevolent God. God's grace comes to us when we ask for it in the simple prayer of confession. The apostle John said, "Whoever confesses that Jesus is the Son of God, God abides in him, and he in God" (1 John 4:15).

Salvation is the work of God both in its inception and in its continuance. The coming of Christ saves us, but the abiding of God within us keeps us saved. Salvation is the life of God living in the one who confessed Jesus as the Christ. Since this is where the Christian life starts, it must be the place where Christian praying begins; for the first premise of prayer is the acknowledgment of a higher power who can be invoked to intervene in our personal affairs. This is what acknowledging the lordship of Jesus accomplishes. God is entreated to rule in us.

The prayer God requires from the sinner is a two-fold prayer of confession: first of all, the confession that the petitioner is a sinner. This prayer doesn't require a specific confession of individual sins because few, if any, have memories good enough to recall all of their acts of self-will.

Secondly, this prayer contains the confession that Jesus is his or her Lord. The Bible merely calls for the sinner to confess Christ Jesus. Paul summarized it by saying, "If you confess with your mouth the Lord Jesus and believe in your heart that God has raised Him from the dead, you will be saved. For with the heart one believes unto righteousness, and with the mouth confession is made unto salvation" (Romans 10:9,10).

If ever I saw a vivid illustration of the need for both a confession of faith and the confession of sin in order to come into a vital relationship with Jesus Christ, it was in the life of Henry. Although he was a young, energetic man who seemed to find it easy to confess Jesus Christ as his Savior, Henry didn't have inner peace or evidence of Christ's joy in his life. He would attend a men's prayer meeting, but his prayer would be empty and hollow.

He was faithful to church services and work programs and always projected a life of near perfection. There was, however, no spiritual fruit to be seen in his life. On several occasions I probed to see if he had actually confessed to Christ that he was a sinner, but he always resisted me.

In the mercy of God, he had a frightening experience in an airplane that made him face the nearness of death. He came to the church, and although his prayer was motivated by fear, he confessed not only that he was a sinner but that he was involved in some major sin.

Time proved that it was more than a scared prayer. His life was changed. He forsook his sin and found a sweet relationship with God. His problem all along had been unconfessed sin, and the Bible still declares, "But your iniquities have separated you from your God; and your sins have hid His face from you, so that He will not hear" (Isaiah 59:2).

Confession for Cleansing

To the maturing Christian, John says, "If we confess our sins, He is faithful and just to forgive us our sins and to cleanse us from all unrighteousness" (1 John 1:9). Sometimes well-meaning Christian workers quote this verse to sinners while seeking to lead them into conversion, but no sinner desires or dares to face God's justice; a sinner needs and pleads God's mercy.

The believer, however, dares to call upon God's faithfulness to His covenants and His justice as exemplified at Calvary. Having confessed the lordship of Christ Jesus, the believer enters into a family relationship with God that establishes rules of conduct, with incumbent penalties for disobedience and blessings for obedience. This is amply illustrated in the Old Testament law, which brought Israel into a covenant relationship with God. The law is quite equally divided into blessings and curses—blessings to the obedient and curses to the disobedient. This same principle is carried into the New Testament, which teaches that obedience to God's Word brings believers into the blessings of God's love, but disobedience brings believers under God's chastisement and eventually under His judgment.

Disobedience to God's Word and will is sin. The Bible says, "Whoever commits sin also commits lawlessness, and sin is lawlessness" (1 John 3:4). Sin is disobedience; it is not so much the rebellious deed as it is the desire to rebel and insist upon our own way. Sin is the exercise of the self-will against the known will of God—as illustrated in Adam when he deliberately and rebelliously ate of the forbidden fruit.

30

Sin is common to the human race—even to Christians. The Bible declares, "If we say that we have no sin, we deceive ourselves, and the truth is not in us" (1 John 1:8). While the work of the cross broke the power of sin and fully paid the penalty of sin, it did not eradicate the presence of sin either in the world or in the lives of those who have confessed Christ Jesus as Lord.

We live in a sinful environment; we reside in an unredeemed body; even our minds maintain much of their former corruption. Provisionally, we are fully redeemed when we confess Jesus as our Lord, but the work of redemption— buying back—is progressive. Paul explained it this way: "Do not be conformed to this world, but be transformed by the renewing of your mind, that you may prove what is that good and acceptable and perfect will of God" (Romans 12:2). Salvation calls for us to refuse continually to conform to the standards set by the world system and to renew our minds perpetually—retrain our thought patterns—to conform to the will of God.

It would be wonderful if all Christians scored 100 percent in this daily task, but that isn't realistic. We fail in a thousand different ways, and every failure is sin—a transgression of God's expressed will. These accumulated sins can become such a weight of guilt as to destroy our joy, disturb our peace, and disrupt our fellowship with God; but there is no sensible reason to allow these daily sins to accumulate. John wrote: "My little children, these things I write to you, so that you may not sin. And if anyone sins, we have an Advocate with the Father, Jesus Christ the righteous" (1 John 2:1). He says, "Don't sin; but if you do sin, God has made provision to handle that sin."

What is that provision? The finished work of Christ. How do we enter into that provision? Not by again repeating the sinner's prayer. Our sin has not renounced the lordship of Jesus in our lives; it has only temporarily set it aside in one area of our living. The Christian's answer to sin is the confession of sin. God's answer to confessed sin is the removal of that sin.

This principle is illustrated beautifully in the Old Testament provision of the scapegoat (see Leviticus 16). Two goats were presented to the Lord and the hands of the priest were laid on them while the sins of Israel were confessed. Lots were cast, and one of the goats was offered on the brazen altar as a sin offering, while a chosen

Cleansing for the Christian demands that sin be called sin.

representative led the other goat into the wilderness far from the children of Israel. As the goat was led away, the Israelites visualized their sins being taken out of the camp never again to be seen or remembered. Christ is both the animal slain for the sins of the world and the One upon whom all of our sins and iniquities were laid; He bore them out of our lives, out of our sight, never again to be remembered against us.

This is why God can say, "If we confess our sins, He is faithful and just to forgive us our sins and to cleanse us from all unrighteousness" (1 John 1:9). Cleansed sin is removed sin.

We might better understand this verse if we translated it, "If we confess as sin what God calls sin...." Cleansing for the Christian demands that sin be called sin. But that word tends to stick in our throats, scratch our tongues, and lodge in our teeth. It just does not want to come out. Because we do not like to admit overt rebellion against God, we use such euphemistic terms as error, human frailty, or weakness; but the bare fact is that we have sinned. Until we can bring ourselves to call sin by that hideous name, we will remain defiled by it, for "He is faithful and just to forgive us our sins and to cleanse us...." The divine provision is for sin, not for errors in judgment or behavior.

Some years ago, the Holy Spirit put His convicting finger upon a practice in my life. Under the weight of conviction, I said that I was sorry; but with that came verbal rationalizations, explaining to God that it was a common practice, that it was not really harmful, that it was a form of relaxation from the stress of ministry. My apologies were followed by repeat performances, which, in turn, brought the conviction of the Holy Spirit on my life.

One day a woman in my congregation stepped into my

office to say, "Pastor, I am here praying in the prayer room. I feel that God wants me to tell you something, but it doesn't make any sense to me. Perhaps it will make sense to you."

"Fine," I said. "Give me God's message."

She said, "God says that this is the last time He will ever speak to you about it."

With that she closed the office door and left. I knew all too well what God meant. He was tired of playing games with me. He was about to abandon me to my own will in the matter. I dropped to my knees and tried to repent of this "error," but nothing happened. After it became obvious that none of my religious phrases and pious pleading would satisfy either God or my own heart, I prayed, "Lord, please help me to see this thing as You see it."

God answered me almost immediately. Inwardly, I sensed a horror, a revulsion, and a feeling of absolute filth. God was making me aware of what sin was like to Him. I never want to repeat that experience. I am not skillful enough in the use of words to communicate to another what I felt. My little "error" was horrible to God's nature. There are no small unrighteousnesses. If Isaiah is correct in announcing, "But we are all like an unclean thing, and all our righteousnesses are like filthy rags" (Isaiah 64:6a), what must our *unrighteousness* be like to Him whom we have acknowledged as our Lord?

I wept openly before God. I apologized for offending Him, and I asked His forgiveness for dealing so lightly with the Spirit's conviction; but I felt as if I were dangled over hell on a barbecue spit. I was allowed not only to feel some of God's revulsion to sin, but to taste some of His wrath, for Paul said, "The wrath of God is revealed from heaven against all ungodliness and unrighteousness of men, who suppress the truth in unrighteousness" (Romans 1:18).

I could not find relief in my spirit regardless of what I prayed. Finally, in near desperation, I stopped using the more gentle words and phrases for my behavior and dared to call it sin. Something wonderful happened within me when I confessed my sin. It was like an instrumentalist finding the key in which the rest of the orchestra members were playing. I found my spirit in harmony with God. Music was once again flowing within. The mere confessing as sin what God had called sin brought me cleansing, forgiveness, and harmony with God.

In retrospect, I wonder why it took me so long to call it sin, for God's Word clearly declares, "All unrighteousness is sin" (1 John 5:17a). I, like others, tried to cover my sin, but the Bible warns, "He who covers his sins will not prosper, but whoever confesses and forsakes them will have mercy" (Proverbs 28:13).

David taught us this principle. After his heinous double sin of adultery and murder, he had to deal with God. He wrote, "I acknowledged my sin to You, and my iniquity I have not hidden. I said, 'I will confess my transgressions to the Lord,' and You forgave the iniquity of my sin. Selah" (Psalm 32:5). In this lesson on how to get back into the favor of God, David used the three most common Old Testament words for behavior that separates us from God: sin, transgression, and iniquity. They may refer to a single act, but they are not synonymous terms. Sin is the inner desire of self-will versus God's will; it is the intent. Transgression is the violation of God's command; it is the act. But iniquity is that within us which excuses our sin and makes allowances for it; iniquity is the cover-up.

Our lives need a complete cleansing from all three of these, for the desire, the deed, and the duplicity all interact. By God's grace, the promise given to the person who will confess all of this as defiling sin is: "He is faithful and just to forgive...and to cleanse us from all unrighteousness." Correct confession of sin always brings complete cleansing from that sin.

Although there should not be a finalized ritual to prayer, it is likely that very early in our prayer time we will find ourselves praying the prayer of confession of sin that brings us cleansing and purity; for when we deal with God, He deals with us as well. One of His beneficial dealings is conviction of sin. When this confessed sin is removed, we are able to enjoy the holy nature of God.

After sin is confessed, we should confess the cleansing that God has promised. Faith thanks and praises God for His

> While confession admits being wrong, it also accepts being changed.

forgiving grace. We need not deal further with the filth in our lives; all confessed sin is forgiven and flushed from our lives much as running tap water flushes out the dirty contents of a cup that is held under its flow.

Cleansed! What a relief. What a restoration. It is as though we had never been defiled. God removes the filth of sin from us and erases heaven's record of that sin. The cleansed cup can be returned to the table and no one can tell which cup had been dirty.

Confession of sin is gloriously positive. It effects a change. It deals positively with a dangerous negative. While confession admits being wrong, it also accepts being changed. It settles the rebellion of the heart and brings atonement for the action. Confession places the sin upon Jesus, and He has dealt so conclusively with sin by His death and resurrection that, instead of drawing back from us, He draws us close to Himself in the embrace of reuniting love and fellowship. What a marvelous place to be when praying to God!

Confession for Commitment

Once sin is settled, we enjoy fellowship with God. The beginning of this fellowship is clearly stated as, "He who comes to God must believe that He is, and that He is a rewarder of those who diligently seek Him" (Hebrews 11:6*b*). Both of these truths have been realized by the forgiven one, and in vocal declaration of these truths, faith is stirred into action. Prayer to God is in itself an admission that we believe He exists. Just the breathing of the name "Jesus" causes our spirits to respond to His person much like speaking the name of a loved one brings memories, excitement, and awareness to our souls. God is real, and prayer is a vocalization of that reality.

Sometimes prayer is little more than breathing the name of God, and then enjoying the response of God whispering our names back to us. Is it not when we are in prayer that we realize, "The Lord your God in your midst, the Mighty One, will save; He will rejoice over you with gladness, He will quiet you with His love, He will rejoice over you with singing" (Zephaniah 3:17)? Surely if God can delight over us enough to burst forth into song, it would not be out of order for us to delight similarly over Him. Some of the most beautiful confessions of God's being burst forth within me melodiously. I usually awaken with a song in my spirit, and when my conscious mind is not occupied, it often returns to singing. Song is more than the recitation of a creed of belief; it also releases loving emotions as further attestation to our confidence that "God is...." It's no wonder that more songs have been composed with God as the theme than all other themes put together. Singing these songs about God can be a marvelous and prayerful confession of our faith in God.

Hebrews 11:6 insists not only that we who come to God in prayer must believe that He is. We are also to believe "that He is a rewarder of

> He has promised to reward such a seeker with His presence.

those who diligently seek Him." He is God; He is approachable; He is a rewarder. Not one of us needs to approach God in terror and fear, for He reveals Himself as the rewarder of those who search for Him. This may, of course, indicate that He will grant our petitions, but we will discuss that later.

When a lonely, hard-working prospector searches the desert for gold, his reward is a vein of gold. When a young woman seeks a husband, her reward is marriage. Similarly, the greatest reward a seeker of God can find is God Himself. The Shulamite woman said: "By night...I sought the one I love; I sought him, but I did not find him. 'I will rise now,' I said, 'and go about the city; in the streets and in the squares I will seek the one I love!' I sought him, but I did not find him... When I found the one I love, I held him and would not let him go" (Song of Solomon 3:1,2,4a). Since this was written, millions of Christians have experienced the same intense pursuit of God. They've often searched in the wrong places, their desire intensifying with the prolonged search.

Sometimes we seek God in service; other times, in ritual, but these channels rarely satisfy our spiritual longings. When we enter the prayer chamber—coming by way of the cross—our pursuit—now a consuming passion—can be satisfied in the realized presence of God. How lovingly He has promised to reward such a seeker with His own presence. Like lovers who have long been separated, the union and communion that flow when God is found are beyond description. Words prove to be insufficient; they give place to touch and nearly inaudible sighs of pleasure. "I have found Him" is the cry of the heart; "I love You" is the expression of the lips, and both the seeker and the One sought are rewarded.

When He was with us on earth, Jesus said, "I say to you, ask, and it will be given to you; seek, and you will find; knock, and it will be opened to you. For everyone who asks receives, and he who seeks finds, and to him who knocks it will be opened" (Luke 11:9,10). Perhaps asking refers to needed things; perhaps seeking concerns service; but knocking is obviously the expression of a desire for entrance. The reward for a knocker is an opened door, and Jesus promises that all persistent knockers will be admitted to His presence. This calls for more than a "word of prayer"; it calls for prayer that knocks on heaven's door until the Resident inside opens that door to give us an entrance. Sometimes one knock gains an admission, but at other times the praying must become persistent.

We have all quoted the old Scottish proverb, "Open confession is good for the soul." But confession involves more than quoting the proverb. We must either confess Christ Jesus as our Lord or confess our sins to the Lord Jesus Christ. Confession is coming to terms with God through Jesus. It is not bargaining with God, nor is it begging God. It is meeting the terms of His contract with us. When we confess His Son, we are saved. When we confess our sins, we are cleansed, and when we confess His existence and rewarding nature, we ascend to glory, brought into His presence.

At the moment, this is optional for mankind. Millions of persons ignore the lordship of Jesus Christ deliberately and deny the existence of God. They lose the promised benefits such confession would bring. But there is coming a day when "at the name of Jesus every knee should bow, of those in heaven, and of those on earth, and of those under the earth, and that every tongue should confess that Jesus Christ is Lord, to the glory of God the Father" (Philippians 2:10,11). Forced confessions lead to punishment and separation from God. It is only the voluntary confession that leads to righteousness and intimate relationship with God.

Those who have confessed their way into such a relationship find the next step in prayer most beneficial, for they discover that prayer is the channel for petition. They can embrace the admonition, "Be anxious for nothing, but in everything by prayer and supplication, with thanksgiving, let your requests be made known to God" (Philippians 4:6).

For Reflection

1. Do you see confession to God as negative or positive?
2. If you see it as positive, what results can you expect from honest confession?
3. Does it increase your faith to confess who God is when talking to Him?

rayer Ascends As the Channel for Petition

Seven times (the Bible's number of perfection) Solomon's name is mentioned in the New Testament. Jesus said, "The queen of the South will rise up in the judgment with this generation and condemn it, for she came from the ends of the earth to hear the wisdom of Solomon; and indeed a *greater than Solomon* is here" (Matthew 12:42, italics added). It is Solomon's position, not his person, that the New Testament exalts. While his character eroded to a level that could never be accepted as exemplary, his royalty, his wisdom, his wealth, and his reign over a united kingdom are a remarkable type of Christ Jesus our Lord. The comparison, of course, is not that of equality but of similarity. Solomon was wise; Christ is all-wise. Solomon reigned over a united kingdom; Jesus is "King of kings and Lord of lords" (Revelation 19:16).

It is interesting to note that in declaring Himself to be greater than Solomon, Jesus referred to the visit of the queen of Sheba, who traveled a great distance to communicate with Solomon. She came to learn; she asked questions, and Solomon answered. What a beautiful type of prayer. We, too, must traverse the distance between earth and heaven to come into the presence of our Lord; there we must expose openly to Him the questions, needs, and deep longings of our hearts. There is nothing that is unknown to Him, and He can give us direction, guidance, and knowledge that will satisfy the needs of our lives.

In the Old Testament account of this visit, we read, "King Solomon gave the queen of Sheba all she desired, whatever she asked, besides what Solomon had given her according to the royal generosity" (1 Kings 10:13*a*). As Solomon showed her the splendor of his capital, it is likely that he invited her to

39

ask for anything she desired. Seeing so many things of irresistible charm, she likely asked for much, quite often. It is possible that she came to the point where she was embarrassed to ask for more; yet she could not conceal her continuing desires, and Solomon, sensitive to these feelings, granted her requests—and more.

Besides what she asked for, hinted at, and merely looked at with longing, Solomon "gave her of his royal generosity." The literal Hebrew is "according to the hand of King Solomon," indicating that his lavish generosity was commensurate with his unparalleled riches.

If the Lord we fellowship with in prayer is "greater than Solomon," we should expect His generosity and compassion to be greater than Solomon's. The New Testament writers indicate that we can expect exuberant responses to our petitions. John wrote, "Now this is the confidence that we have in Him, that if we ask anything according to His will, He hears us. And if we know that He hears us, whatever we ask, we know that we have the petitions that we have asked of Him" (1 John 5:14,15). And Dr. Luke quotes Jesus as having promised, "I say to you, ask, and it will be given to you; seek, and you will find; knock, and it will be opened to you. For everyone who asks receives, and he who seeks finds, and to him who knocks it will be opened" (Luke 11:9,10).

Paul, however, lifts us to the heights of expectancy in his great benediction: "Now to Him who is able to do exceedingly abundantly above all that we ask or think, according to the power that works in us, to Him be glory in the church by Christ Jesus to all generations, forever and ever. Amen" (Ephesians 3:20,21). What superabundance has been pledged to us: "Whatever we ask...we have of Him;" "ask and it will be given to you;" and "exceedingly abundantly above all that we ask or think." The queen of Sheba certainly had nothing on us, for while she received from the bounty of Solomon's provision, we receive from the immeasurable abundance of God's ability to provide.

The Prelude to Prayer

Far more valuable than the teachings of either John or Paul are the principles of prayer that the "greater than Solomon" exemplified and expressed while He was here on the earth with us. Jesus demonstrated the purpose, privilege, and power of prayer, but He also taught us that we have access to this same channel of communication with God. Actually, there are two groups of teachings on prayer in the three-and-one-half years of Christ's ministry. The first is in the Sermon on the Mount, about halfway through the second year of His ministry. This was given to the crowd gathered to hear His teaching, and it taught them the value of private prayer without the vain repetitions the heathen used. It also contained the model prayer, which we so often call the "Lord's Prayer."

The second group of teachings on prayer comes at the end of Jesus' life. Most of it was given in the last days, and much of it was shared on the very eve of the last tragic day. These words were not spoken to the crowds but to the small group of disciples. Jesus talked one way to the multitude and quite a different way to those who had separated themselves from the crowd to come into the inner circle in fellowship with Himself.

Before looking at four fundamental principles that Jesus taught about prayer in the Upper Room, let me point out a radical statement that precedes the teaching. A few days before, Jesus had said, "If anyone desires to come after Me, let him deny himself, and take up his cross, and follow Me" (Matthew 16:24). These words need to be written across all the promises regarding prayer that Jesus made in the Upper Room.

The basic condition to these promises is a life fully surrendered to the will of God, a purpose completely dedicated to God's purposes, and a will wholly subject to God's will. The person who will follow Jesus to Gethsemane, Gabbatha, and Golgotha may ask what he chooses to ask, and that thing will come to pass.

> Persons who will not allow the cross to become a daily routine, live in their own will with only occasional excursions into the will of God.

The prime reason so many people do not have power in prayer is simply because they have sidestepped the cross. They are unwilling to identify continually with the death of Jesus. They do not choose to be like Paul, who testified, "I have been crucified with Christ; it is no longer I who live, but Christ lives in me" (Galatians 2:20), and "I die daily" (1 Corinthians 15:31*b*). Persons who will not allow the cross to become a daily routine, live in their own will with only occasional excursions into the will of God. Their prayer, however subconscious it may be, is "nevertheless, not Thy will, but mine be done." Prayer, to them, becomes a directing of God.

By explanation and by example, Jesus taught that if a person follows the Master's guidance quietly and resolutely—nothing extreme, fanatical, or morbid, just a quiet going where the inner voice leads plainly day by day—he will be startled to find an utterly new meaning of prayer.

This principle is demonstrated amply in the life of John; he and his brother James pled with Jesus for the privilege of sitting at the right and left hand of Christ when He

John did not sit at Christ's right hand, but he did stand at His bleeding side...

came into His kingdom. He even had his mother intercede with Jesus to grant this favor. Jesus had to explain that neither son realized what he was asking for. In the discourse that followed, He exposed their hearts as desiring power and authority to rule over people.

After John witnessed the arrest, trial, and crucifixion of Jesus—being the one disciple who stayed with Jesus to the very end—John was softened in his personal ambition. Knowing this, Jesus dared to commit the care of His mother into John's hands. The lust for rule over people had been replaced with a willingness to serve those whom Christ loved. John did not sit at Christ's right hand, but he did stand at His bleeding side, with such identification that he became "the apostle of love."

The responses of people to Jesus while He was on the earth seem to parallel subsequent responses to Him since His ascension. Multitudes thronged Jesus, eager for the loaves and fishes and for His teaching about provision from God. Of these, seventy were willing to follow Jesus into power ministries as they toured the cities of Judea healing the sick and casting out devils. Twelve of the seventy followed Jesus day-by-day, enjoying fellowship with Him; but only three of these disciples went with Jesus into the garden for a night of intercession (and they slept through it). Of these three, only John followed Jesus all the way to Calvary. It seems that the more the attention is turned from us to God, the fewer the persons who are willing to get involved.

Just as the queen of Sheba received nothing until she was in a cordial and personal relationship with Solomon, so the Christian who wants prayers answered will have to learn to come into that intimate relationship that begins at the cross. There at the cross, personal ambition, pride, selfishness, and greed die so the higher life of Christ may be revealed in our prayers.

At the cross, we learn that prayer is not a fetish; it is fellowship with God. It is not a charm; it is communion with Christ. The uncrucified person may view prayer as a magic formula guaranteed to get mystical results, but he or she will soon discover that prayer reduced to a recipe will not work. Prayer is not the key that unlocks the doors of heaven or moves the hand of God; Christ is! It was neither the queen's request nor her desires that produced Solomon's gifts. Everything came from the hand of the king. Similarly, our prayers may indicate what we want, but any realized desires are bestowed on us by the gracious hand of Christ. The more we ask in accordance to His will, the more He will grant to us in response to our petitions. This is why it is important that our wills, wants, and wishes go to the cross before our petitions go to the throne.

The Promise of Prayer

It is evident that the greatest teachings of Jesus were not given to the multitudes; they were reserved for the more intimate circle of followers. Christ's teaching on prayer given to His disciples in the Upper Room is far deeper and richer than those given in the Sermon on the Mount.

John records this higher teaching on prayer in chapters 14 through 17 of his Gospel. It begins with Christ's revelation, "I am the way, the truth, and the life. No one comes to the Father except through Me" (John 14:6). And then Jesus told them, "Most assuredly, I say to you, he who believes in Me, the works that I do he will do also; and greater works than these he will do, because I go to My Father." Immediately, He added, "And whatever you ask in My name, that I will do, that the Father may be glorified in the Son. If you ask anything in My name, I will do it" (John 14:12-14).

This was startling to the disciples, who knew little of prayer beyond the Lord's prayer. Jesus admitted this when He said, "In that day you will ask Me nothing. Most assuredly, I say to you, whatever you ask the Father in My name He will give you. Until now you have asked nothing in My name. Ask, and you will receive, that your joy may be full" (John 16:23,24). The disciples had depended upon Jesus to "pray them through," but now the Master was authorizing them to go directly to the Father in the name of Jesus and lay their petitions boldly before Him.

Jesus told them that He was the way to the Father, that they could enter into greater works of prayer than He had because He was going to the Father as their intercessor, and that He was authorizing them to approach the Father in prayer with assurance that their requests would be answered. This is still the great promise of prayer for the inner circle of believers who have come into a warm personal relationship with Jesus.

When my daughters reached their teen years, I was a busy pastor of a growing church. Attempting to maintain a sense of availability to these three precious ones, I gave each of them a key to the church and to my office. While church members had to have an appointment and come to me through my secretary, my daughters were instructed to bypass the secretary, put their keys into the lock on the door, and come in to see their father. They always had priority because they had the closest relationship with me.

Isn't this what Jesus meant? Those who have the most personal relationship with Him have the most immediate access of prayer. Anything they ask is granted. Their petition is akin to the request "Please pass the potatoes" during a Thanksgiving dinner. There is never any question about whether or not the potatoes will be passed; their presence on the table means that they are available. The petition is but a polite way of saying that you cannot reach what you now desire. The person closest to the potatoes will pass them to the petitioner.

The Father has provided all things needed by His family. He will not thrust these things upon the children, but He delights to serve them up as soon as they are requested. Such access to divine provision has been granted to us that our "joy may be full" (John 16:24*b*). God does not want us to lack anything in His service any more than I want my secretary to function without proper equipment and supplies.

This promise is a conditional promise. God's word, through Jesus, is that when we ask, He supplies. It is our call that prompts His answer. Prayerlessness will not only mean powerlessness in service, but it will result in shortages of supplies. While it is obvious that God knows our needs long before we express them to Him in prayer, for His own purposes He has commanded us to ask, to petition, to pray.

The Prerequisite in Prayer

In this final teaching, Jesus expressed at least four prerequisites to effective prayer. In the order that He presented them, they are love, obedience, fruitfulness, and abiding. These are the qualifying classes—the fine print—in the contract of prayer that Jesus was offering.

Almost as soon as Judas left the Upper Room, Jesus said, "A new commandment I give to you, that you have love for one another; **as I have loved you, that you also love one another.** By this all will know that you are My disciples, if you have love for one another" (John 13:34,35). Three more times that evening Jesus told them that love was a commandment (14:15; 15:12,17). Loving those who have come into fellowship with Christ—the other disciples—is a test of discipleship, a test of obedience, and a condition for answered prayer.

In the Sermon on the Mount, which the disciples heard, Jesus taught that if anyone coming to the altar for worship or

45

petition realized that he had a broken relationship with another person, he was to go and be reconciled with that person before returning to offer anything to God. (See Matthew 5:23,24.) On another occasion, He stated, "Whenever you stand praying, if you have anything against anyone, forgive him, that your Father in heaven may also forgive you your trespasses. But if you do not forgive, neither will your Father in heaven forgive your trespasses" (Mark 11:25,26).

Horizontal relationships must be preserved if the vertical relationship is to be productive. Our relationship with God cannot exceed our rela-

> **Much unproductive prayer can be traced to an unloving, unforgiving nature.**

tionship with our fellow disciples. John caught this teaching, for he later wrote, "If someone says, 'I love God,' and hates his brother, he is a liar; for he who does not love his brother whom he has seen, how can he love God whom he has not seen? And this commandment we have from Him; that he who loves God must love his brother also" (1 John 4:20,21). Much unproductive prayer can be traced to an unloving, unforgiving nature.

I believe that Della is a prime example of this. How she would cry out to God for her children! She often asked me to join her in these prayers. There appeared to be no answer to these intercessions. The heavens seemed closed to her prayers. As I got to know Della better, I found a deep anger in her toward her husband. It was almost to the point of hatred. I began to systematically work on this whenever I was around her.

Slowly the Lord melted Della's heart until the resentment poured out, and God's love poured into her for her disappointing husband. Almost amazingly God began to work in the lives of her sons. The son of her prime concern is now saved, filled with the spirit, working on the worship team of his church, and studying for the ministry.

The second prerequisite that Jesus emphasized is obedience. He said, "He who has My commandments and keeps them, it is he who loves Me. And he who loves Me will be loved by My Father, and I will love him and manifest Myself to him" (John 14:21). Love for Christ is not measured by tears, shouts, or even service. Jesus placed the measurement of our love for Himself in the level of our obedience to His commandments. None can live in open rebellion to the known will of God and expect to have open access to God through prayer. Petitions to a holy God should come from a holy people or, at least, from a people being made holy in their obedience to the divine commands.

Jesus declared that implicit obedience is the appointed route to abiding in the love of God the Father and God the Son. "If you keep My com-

> Love for Christ is not measured by tears, shouts, or even service.

mandments, you will abide in My love, just as I have kept My Father's commandments and abide in His love," He told the disciples (John 15:10). God told King Saul through the prophet Samuel: "Behold, to obey is better than sacrifice, and to heed than the fat of rams. For rebellion is as the sin of witchcraft, and stubbornness is as iniquity and idolatry" (1 Samuel 15:22*b*,23*a*). We cannot practice witchcraft and pray successfully to God. If we are to expect our prayers to become prevailing prayers, we must submit our wills to the known will of God and walk in obedience to His commands.

Jesus so clearly said, "I am the way, the truth, and the life: no man cometh unto the Father, but by me" (John 14:6). We have no access to God but Jesus, and His route is truth and life. Unfortunately, some, like Marvin in the following story, don't want to deal with truth. They just want to come to God.

Every time Marvin seemed to be close to breaking through to God, he would withdraw for a while. He searched for God outside the church by reading books of eastern religions. For a while he dabbled in the occult trying to satisfy his heart's cry after God, but he only found more misery—not peace.

After messing up his life for a season, Marvin came back to church and confessed his sins to God. When he faced the truth about himself and about God, he had a glorious encounter with Christ. He discovered that *finding* God was not too difficult.

Surrendering his life to the Lord was the great impediment.

Jesus' third prerequisite to answered prayer was fruitfulness. In John 15, Jesus illustrated this in terms of a grapevine. He called Himself the main stalk, or the vine, and named us the branches. Any fruit produced grows on the branches, but the branches must remain in a vital, living connection with the vine in order to bear the grapes. The flow of life which produces the fruit must come from the roots, through the vine, and out through the branches. Anything that disrupts this flow will prevent fruitfulness. Jesus said it so simply: "Abide in Me, and I in you. As the branch cannot bear fruit of itself, unless it abides in the vine, neither can you, unless you abide in Me. I am the vine, you are the branches. He who abides in Me, and I in him, bears much fruit; for without Me you can do nothing" (John 15:4,5).

If Jesus was accurate in saying, "Without Me you can do nothing," then productive prayer must be done with Him—not without Him. The faith and spiritual vitality necessary for prayer to be productive flows from Christ to the praying believer by action of the Spirit. We cannot produce this, but we can channel it if we remain in an abiding relationship with Jesus. Anything that would sever us from this relationship must be treated as sin—confessed immediately and forsaken if we hope to be fruitful in the Master's vineyard.

The branch, of course, cannot choose what to produce. It will bring forth fruit always consistent to the attached vine. The nature of Jesus will develop on the branch of the abiding Christian as surely as grapes grow on the branch that abides in the vine. It is this fruit that Jesus yearns for in believers. He told His disciples, "You did not choose Me, but I chose you and appointed you that you should go and bear fruit, and that your fruit should remain, *that whatever you ask the Father in My name He may give you*" (John 15:16, italics added). Fruitfulness and resourceful prayer are intricately bound together.

Jesus gave a fourth prerequisite to answered prayer: abiding. It is interwoven with fruitfulness. The emphasis here, however, is less on the end and more on the means. As we live in union and communion with Jesus, a consistent flow of the Holy Spirit brings the nature of Jesus into our lives. We do

48

not get "plugged in" to Jesus on Sunday like an electrical appliance; we grow out of Him day and night like the limb of a tree. We not only work in Him; we rest in Him, for the very life-flow of God is dependent upon this vital connection between the believer and Christ Jesus.

To be severed from this relationship is to wilt and die, for Jesus said, "If anyone does not abide in Me, he is cast out as a branch and is withered; and they gather them and throw them into the fire, and they are burned" (John 15:6). The penalty for nonabiding is permanent. In contrast to this, the person who has learned to remain in the love of Christ, whatever adjustments in life-style it may entail, is offered the highest reward of prayer—answers! Jesus said, "If you abide in Me, and My words abide in you, you will ask what you desire, and it shall be done for you" (John 15:7). It is unlikely that the abiding Christian would ask for anything outside of the will of God, for his or her very prayer will be inspired by the abiding Spirit of Christ.

The Provision in Prayer

The person who has met the prerequisites Jesus gave for productive prayer will discover the enormous provision Jesus gave in prayer. He said, "Most assuredly, I say to you, whatever you ask the Father in My name He will give you" (John 16:23b), and, "In that day you will ask in My name, and I do not say to you that I shall pray the Father for you" (John 16:26). It seems that Jesus offers two separate provisions in prayer: authority and alternatives.

The authority that we have in prayer is unlimited, for Jesus says repeatedly we are to ask in His name. We are not speaking merely as petitioning saints, but we are addressing the Father in the name, in the authority, of His Son. This is a granted "power of attorney" that allows us to use the name of Jesus as though it were our own name.

Many years ago, as a young preacher, I was involved in the construction of a new church structure. I was acting as the contractor for the job, while the men of the congregation were doing all of the labor. A member of that congregation, and a personal friend of mine, owned the largest construction firm in that tri-city area. Years before, while we were both in college, we had lived next door to each other in a duplex.

Our building program was several months along when Don spoke to me after a Sunday morning service. "Pastor," he said, "are you getting builders' discounts from the wholesale outlets in the area?"

"No," I said. "None of the wholesale outlets will sell to me because I don't have a license."

"I was afraid of that," he said. "Tomorrow, I'll pick you up at about ten o'clock."

That next day, he took me to every wholesale outlet in the area. Because of the volume of business he represented, he was waited on immediately—by the manager. Calling each manager by name, Don introduced me. Then he said, "From now on this man is to be considered as Don Speer. He represents me. Anything he chooses to purchase is to be put on my account, and he will sign my name for me."

For the next two years, whenever I walked into one of those outlets, I was treated with the same courtesy given to Don Speer. I received preferential treatment, even though I often wanted only a keg of nails. It was not what I bought, but what Don Speer bought that made it practical for them to cater to me over other customers. I had the right to do business in the name of Don Speer, for I was functioning under his name.

Isn't this what Jesus offers to us when He says we can "ask the Father in My name"? We have an authority in the heavens, because Jesus chose to leave a power-of-attorney with us. **We are commissioned to do business for Him as though He Himself were here transacting that business.** What a provision!

But there is a second factor in this promise that sometimes nearly negates the first. **We have the alternative of choosing what to ask for.** Jesus said, "Whatever you ask the Father in My name He will give you" (John 16:23). Just as I never had to contact Don Speer to determine what I could purchase in his name, so we have an open opportunity to pick and choose what we intend to ask the Father to do in the name of Jesus. This level of choice calls for true spiritual maturity, for children tend to lavish everything selfishly upon themselves when granted unlimited options.

When we completed the building for which I purchased materials in the name of another (of course, the church reimbursed him for purchases made in his name), God gave us a beautiful visitation of His presence that lasted for several years. Our congregation became a praying group of people, and the answers to prayer were quite well-known in the community.

One day in my study, as I was in prayer, the Lord gave me a vision. In this revelation, I saw my congregation in a very large store stocked with almost everything imaginable. The showcases on the main floor were filled with dime-store trinkets, but the shelves on the walls held costly items. I saw my congregation picking up the baubles excitedly from the showcases, while ignoring the more costly merchandise on shelves above them.

"Look higher," I cried out. "The best is above us. Don't settle for the knickknacks. God has far more wonderful things available for the asking."

It was as though they were deaf to my voice. None turned away from the things closest at hand. No one even looked up. In the vision, I broke into tears, and when I came out of the vision, I was sitting with my hands covering my face. I was sobbing almost uncontrollably. That congregation had learned to pray in the name of Jesus until they could have had anything they had desired, but I was never able to raise those desires to greater things in God.

How it must grieve the heart of God to see us use our great authority in prayer for selfish ends and greedy purposes—like the teen who wastes his

> Misuse of God's provisions will bring spiritual poverty to any of us.

inheritance on fun and foolishness and then can't afford to go on to college. Christians play the prodigal without ever entering into open sin. Misuse of God's provisions will bring spiritual poverty to any of us. James says, "You ask and do not receive, because you ask amiss, that you may spend it on your pleasures" (James 4:3). Someone has said this could be translated, "You ask and miss because...." Even though we may get what we ask for, it is possible to have missed the perfect will of God and the higher provision He has made available.

The Pattern of Prayer

Jesus followed His final teaching on prayer with the beautiful high priestly prayer of John 17—perhaps because we tend to enter into spiritual privileges with carnal desires. What a prayer this was! It is far more the "Lord's Prayer" than the pattern of prayer given in the Sermon on the Mount.

It is not within the scope of this book to exegete this amazing prayer of Jesus, but its four major thrusts can form a pattern for our praying. **Christ's first concern was for the glory of God.** In the first, fourth, and fifth verses of this prayer, Jesus declared that He had glorified the Father, and now He petitioned the Father to glorify the Son. The cross was just hours away, and yet Christ's petition was not for alleviation of suffering or for special grace to endure. His concern was that the glory of the Father be seen on earth. Jesus yearned that God's glory be manifested in everything, even in His being made sin for suffering humanity.

How wonderful it is when our petitions to God become more concerned with His glory than with our needs and desires. The highest ministry any of us can enter into is the revelation of the glory of God to our sinful world. None of us should want anything that would diminish the revelation of that glory. That which exalts self will extinguish the light of the glory of God. It is not important that any of us be seen, for we are not the Savior. It is when the Lord is high and lifted up that men are drawn to Him. (See John 12:32.)

In the next portion of the high priestly prayer (John 17:6-8), **Jesus gave a report of His activities on earth to the Father in heaven.** It was brief, for His purpose was not to give the Father "unknown information" but to give an account for the responsibility that had been entrusted to Him.

We, too, are accountable to God. The parable of the talents teaches that responsibility and opportunity will be followed by accountability. Before asking God for something more, we would do well to report to Him what we have done with what

He has already given to us. If we can report faithfulness in small things, we dare to ask and receive greater things from God, but if we have not used properly what He has already given to us, what right have we to ask for more? Jesus reported what He had done in the lives of the disciples that God had given to Him before He petitioned the Father to do greater things in them.

The third division of this high priestly prayer concerned these disciples into whom Jesus had poured His very life. He told the Father, "I pray for them. I do not pray for the world but for those whom You have given Me, for they are Yours" (John 17:9). How amazing that before dying for all mankind, **Jesus prayed specifically for the believers whom the Father had given to Him.**

Paul seemed to learn from this example. In his letters to the churches he said repeatedly that he did not cease to pray for them day and night. Is it possible that in our evangelistic zeal, we pray so often for the lost that we have neither time nor inclination to pray for the saints?

I had an opportunity to see this work in a small way. I was pastor of a congregation in a lumber community. Most of the men of the congregation worked in one of the plywood plants in town. When a recession hit the building trades, all these plants were forced to close. This meant extreme hardship on the employees, and, subsequently, on the church.

I felt a divine faith to plead for the jobs of the men of the congregation. I earnestly prayed that somehow God would spare their jobs for them. The prayer group joined me in this intercession.

Amazingly, every man of the congregation was invited to stay employed as a maintenance worker or on a clean-up crew. When the recession was over, each man was restored to his original job. This became a great testimony to many in our community.

Christ's priority was to pray first for His disciples at hand and then to pray for the disciples who would yet come to Him. **The final portion of His prayer concerned the sheep who were not yet in His fold.** (John 17:20-26) He said, "I do not pray for these alone, but also for those who will believe

53

in Me through their [the present disciples'] word" (John 17:20). Christ obviously had a world vision, but He prayed first for those who would be the channels for reaching others; then He prayed for those who would be reached through their proclamation of the Word.

Our praying becomes more productive when we pray first for those who are sent and then for those to whom they are sent. The Word of God can be empowered by the Spirit of God as a result of prayer by those who aren't directly, actively engaged in proclaiming the Word. It is not by accident that, after urging Christians to put on the whole armor of God, Paul says, "Praying always with all prayer and supplication in the Spirit, being watchful to this end with all perseverance and supplication for all the saints—and for me, that utterance may be given to me, that I may open my mouth boldly to make known the mystery of the gospel" (Ephesians 6:18,19). Paul embraced and taught the pattern of prayer that Jesus used. Perhaps we should also. We should plead for a demonstration of God's glory in our lives, report our accountability, petition for the believers, and intercede for those who have been chosen to preach the gospel throughout the world.

When we move from the Lord's Prayer to the prayer of the Lord recorded in John's Gospel, we move from petitioning God to communicating with God. Our asking gives way to association, and the focus of our prayer moves from ourselves to God Himself.

For Reflection
1. Do you think God gets tired of hearing our "wants lists"?
2. Do we have scriptural authority to petition God for needs? Where is this authority?
3. What prerequisites to effective prayer did Jesus list?

rayer Is the Channel for Communication

Our world has had many outstanding communicators. Philosophers, statesmen, educators, politicians, and salesmen have held audiences captive with their oratorical skills, but the world has never seen a communicator that could equal Christ Jesus. He could hold a crowd so spellbound that the people would stand in the heat of the sun for a full day without eating a bite of food. He could confound the wisest of His enemies, and He never lost a debate with the religious leaders of His day. Still we read that "the common people heard Him gladly" (Mark 12:37*b*).

Jesus was just as good a communicator one-on-one as He was with crowds. Women were comfortable in His presence, and He knew how to communicate with them. Mary sat at His feet, enraptured with His teaching, and the woman of Samaria at Jacob's well was transformed from a sinful woman to a flaming evangelist as the result of a brief conversation with Him. To women, Jesus spoke great truths and communicated spiritual life in an appropriable way.

That Jesus was a great communicator with men is self-evident. Men walked away from their businesses just to be with Him. At His word, governmental workers, religious leaders, fishermen, and tradesmen risked everything to become His followers.

When He was with businessmen, Jesus talked about prop-erty, pearls, and capital; but when He was among farmers, He talked agriculture as though He had been raised on a farm. Fishermen understood His analogies to fishing; and homemak-ers related to His illustrations about leaven, salt, and house-cleaning. It didn't matter to whom Jesus was speaking; He had the ability to communicate spiritual principles in a life-changing way. Little wonder, then, that "the people were astonished at His teaching, for He taught them as one having authority, and not as the scribes" (Matthew 7:28b,29), and that "all bore witness to Him, and marveled at the gracious words which proceeded out of His mouth" (Luke 4:22a). Even the officers who were sent to create an occasion against Jesus, hoping to arrest Him, had to report to the chief priests and Pharisees, "No man ever spoke like this Man" (John 7:46). Jesus was, indeed, the world's greatest communicator.

The twelve men whom Jesus had chosen to accompany Him on His tour of ministry could not help but be deeply impressed with this uncanny ability to communicate. Nonetheless, they never asked Him to teach them how to speak to crowds, adapt their speech to limited groups, or even talk successfully to individuals. They did, however, plead with Jesus to share with them His ability to communicate with God. We read, "Now it came to pass, as He was praying in a certain place, when He ceased, that one of His disciples said to Him, 'Lord, teach us to pray'" (Luke 11:1).

There had to be something in Christ's communication with the Father that arrested the attention of the disciples. They had heard the Pharisees pray in the marketplace for years. They were familiar with the chants of the priests as they went about their prescribed duties. But they saw that Jesus communicated with the Father as if He was talking with a friend. The intimacy of the communication took it out of the realm of the religious and placed it in the realm of relationship. They wanted to learn how to do this.

Furthermore, the disciples had observed that Jesus did not need to be in the temple or the marketplace to pray. He prayed wherever He happened to be. Jesus had learned that prayer is not limited by locale. Jeremiah was imprisoned so he would stop telling the people God's message, yet he was unhindered in communicating with God. Daniel was in a den of lions when his prayer reached the heart of God. And, when Elijah stood on Mount Carmel having "bet his life" that God would answer prayer and destroy the entire system of Baal worship, his prayer was effectual and fervent, producing the intended effect, although he stood as one against 450 priests of Baal.

56

Since prayer is communication with God, and since God is everywhere present at all times, we can talk with God anytime and anywhere. We may pray from a furnished prayer room or from a nearly-bare hospital room. We may call upon God from lives of ease and comfort or from seasons of tension, anxiety or pain. Regardless of race, color, or creed, God has invited us to "call to Me, and I will answer you, and show you great and mighty things, which you do not know" (Jeremiah 33:3).

Prayer Seeks an Audience With God

We will never be effective men and women of prayer if we lose sight of this salient truth. How easy it is to view some of the by-products as the main purpose of prayer. For instance, the Christian who has dedicated himself or herself to prayer dare not view prayer as a do-it-yourself psychological treatment. Prayer is far more than "getting it off your chest." It is higher than talking it out with an unseen partner. Prayer is not merely a purging of the conscience; it is ascending into glory, pursuing an audience with God.

I have discovered, however, that many people prefer an audience with someone else who will pray than have an audience with God themselves. Harold was one of those people. He scheduled counseling session after session through the month. He would go on almost endlessly talking to me about his home problems, his difficulties on his job, and his finances. He would always end the session by saying, "Pastor, please remember me before God when you pray."

After about four such sessions, I had a surprise for him on appointment number five. I suggested that he not sit down when he walked into my office, for we were going to have the counseling in another room. "Harold," I said, "today I want you to have a session with the true Counselor, Jesus Christ. Go to the prayer room for half an hour and talk to Him, and then come back to my office and tell me what He told you."

When he returned, he said, "Pastor, I didn't hear anything from God. It was just a waste of my time."

Harold never scheduled another counseling session, nor did he become one of the praying saints in the congregation. He didn't want to talk to God. He wanted to talk to his pastor. What a sad trade-off! He never learned the marvel of talking with God.

An audience with God—what a privilege! What a purpose! It is splendid to know that God *is*, but to have an audience with God is supreme. Without gaining this audience with God, prayer is meaningless; with it, prayer is potent!

It was this desire for an audience with God that sent the prophets to their watchtowers—or some other place—where they sought an audience with God. Sometimes they called for musicians to play as they prayed; at other times they built altars and offered sacrifices until God spoke to them. Their prayers were not intended to instruct people; their one goal was to get an audience with God. They knew their God, and they understood their calling. Out of their contact with God came communication to the people. There are repeated examples where this contacting of God took days and even weeks, but the prophets would not be content with anything less than a divine contact.

New Testament believers have it much easier. Christ bridged the great gap that had existed between humanity and the Godhead. We read, "Therefore, brethren, having boldness to enter the Holiest by the blood of Jesus, by a new and living way which He consecrated for us, through the veil, that is, His flesh, and having a High Priest over the house of God, let us draw near with a true heart in full assurance of faith, having our hearts sprinkled from an evil conscience and our bodies washed with pure water" (Hebrews 10:19-22). Jesus was far more than an example of prayer. He entered the heavens as our forerunner to make access to God easily and quickly available. We are urged, "Seeing then that we have a great High Priest who has passed through the heavens, Jesus the Son of God... Let us therefore come boldly to the throne of grace" (Hebrews 4:14-16a).

Prayer is no longer an experiment whereby we hope to contact God. Prayer has become a guaranteed route that brings us into God's glorious presence, if we will meet the prescribed conditions.

Perhaps we need to remind ourselves that God is even more eager to have an audience with us than we are to have an audience with Him. The whole plan of redemption was to reunite God's highest creation with its Creator. Ever since Adam forfeited this fellowship, God has been in the process of restoring it. God would still like to walk in the garden with the man and woman He created, just to talk as friends and lovers do. Since this is God's purpose for prayer, shouldn't it also be ours?

Prayer that provides an audience with God must rise a step above mere petition. Remember, Jesus told His disciples, "I say to you, ask, and it will be given to you; seek, and you will find; knock, and it will be opened to you" (Luke 11:9). We ask our petitions; we seek God's person; for did not David cry to God, "When You said, 'Seek My face,' my heart said to You, 'Your face, Lord, I will seek'" (Psalms 27:8).

There is always an element of seek and search in prayer. When our hearts have been completely absorbed in the affairs of our carnal nature, our spirits are forced to remain inactive. Moving from the natural to the spiritual does not always follow a prescribed route. The path that led us to God yesterday may lead us to a dead end today. We may well be forced to try several forms of prayer before we touch the Spirit of God in intimate communion.

Because we are such creatures of habit and so love to make a formula out of prayer, it is easy to endlessly repeat what once worked for us. Dear sister Helen is a prime example of this. In one of

> She was not being led by the Spirit in her prayer life, she was trying to lead the Spirit from her experience levels.

our prayer meetings, there seemed to come a surge of faith in her as she prayed for her husband. She stood to her feet, raised her Bible in the air and proclaimed in a shouting voice, "Lord, I claim his salvation right now!"

In the marvelous grace of God, her husband gave his heart to Jesus the very next Sunday. You can guess what began to happen with great regularity. Helen would stand, raise her

Bible in the air, and make shouting proclamations to God for months. Nothing ever came of them, but that didn't deter her. It had worked once, and she was going to continue her shouting prayer with upraised Bible. She was not being led by the Spirit in her prayer life, she was trying to lead the Spirit from her experience levels.

In God's mercy, we do not have to seek blindly. The Holy Spirit, whom Christ sent, dwells in believers. It is His delight to bring us into the recognized presence of God. He may well inspire the very song that will help us break through the barrier of our flesh, or perhaps He will pray a prayer of confession that releases something that was hindering us. His flow of faith is released fully to God. Prayer is almost fail-proof when the Holy Spirit prays through us. He will get us an audience with the Father.

Prayer Is Conversation With God

Prayer is a means and not an end. It is a vehicle or channel for expressing to God supplication, thanksgiving, petitions, praise and so forth, but prayer is communication—not the thing communicated. A telephone, too, is a means of communication, but what is communicated depends entirely upon the people at the ends of the line. In itself, prayer is not necessarily communion, consecration, concern, or conviction, although prayer may express all of these things. To say, "We have prayed," is little more than to say, "We have talked." What was said when you talked? To whom did you speak? What was the response?

I have been a praying person from my youth. My father was a pastor, and both public and private prayers were part of the environment in which I grew up. I remember hearing a missionary pray in such conversational tones that I was convinced that he knew God and was on speaking terms with Him. It was electrifying. I wanted that kind of praying in my own life. As I learned that true prayer is simply having a conversation with God, my prayer life was transformed. It didn't happen overnight, but I progressed from my recitation of religious phrases to God; I began to talk to Him as the friend He declared Himself to be. As an early by-product of this change, my prayer time ceased being a dreaded religious chore and became an anticipated time of fellowship with God.

I soon discovered that my communication with God had to follow the basic rules of conversation. When we converse with others, we become aware of the other person. We recognize that person's rights, privileges, feelings, and—if we converse long enough—his or her total personality. We really cannot converse with the Lord until we are aware of Him. Therefore, we preface our praying with thanksgiving and praise plus confession of anything that would hinder our prayer. When we phone a friend, we do not begin to converse until the ringing phone is answered; similarly, in prayer we wait until we have gained an audience with God before we begin our vital communication with Him.

Good conversation demands that all affectation and hypocrisy be set aside. Friends do not need the defensive mask of pretense. I found it to my advantage to abandon my formal King James English in talking with God. He doesn't use it, and it was artificial to me. I also began to filter out all the theological phrases and religious jargon I had used in public prayers. God doesn't seem to be impressed with my theological training. Plain conversational language, such as I use with my wife and my daughters, seemed to bring me into a more intimate conversation with God.

Good conversation implies taking turns gracefully. When one person does all the talking, conversation ends and a monologue begins. I had to learn to let God have time to respond to my statements. Our silent waiting for feedback is as much prayer as our vocal entreaties. Good conversation also involves two people pursuing the same subject and pursuing it by turns. We are the listening and speaking members of a team, and we must decide what is relevant and important at the moment. Each person must make use of memory to recall, patience to wait, alertness to jump in, willingness to get out, and—above all—an ability to hold back the disruptive. He must be in tune!

This was a learning experience for me. I was so accustomed to predetermining the subject of my prayer and then pursuing it, that I was shocked to discover that God sometimes wants to

61

discuss something different. I have frequently found it impossible to keep God on my subject! Since His communication to me is far more valuable than any communication I could ever have with Him, I have learned, by trial and error, to flow with His chosen topic and to reserve my subject for another day.

I was flying out to speak at a convention in New York, but my mind was filled with anxiety. I had been invited to become the senior pastor of a great congregation. With my seat reclined to maximum position, I closed my eyes and began to plead with God for direction in this matter. I gave God all the "unknown information" I could think of, but He seemed to ignore everything that I said. Instead, He spoke to me about abiding in Christ. His words were so powerful, they burned deep into my spirit. When I arrived at the convention hall that night, I set aside the message I had prepared and spoke out of my heart the truth God had spoken into my heart on the plane. It proved to be electrifying. I later wrote that truth as my third book, *Let Us Abide.* The entire book had been spoken into my heart during that flight, but it wasn't what I had been praying about. The thousands of people who have been blessed by reading that book can rejoice that God chose the subject of that prayer time. I never did accept the invitation to become the pastor of that congregation.

Conversation with God is a learning experience in which we discover things we did not know about ourselves and about God. Even the Scriptures declare, "The heart is deceitful above all things, and desperately wicked; who can know it? I, the Lord, search the heart; I test the mind, even to give every man according to his ways, according to the fruit of his doings" (Jeremiah 17:9,10). Deep within each of us are things repressed, buried, and forgotten. We can be assured God will bring these to our attention in the course of our conversation with Him. He can show us the way out of them and help us prevent a repeat performance.

Sometimes God's purpose is to communicate truth to us. He helps us see ourselves as He sees us, but it is not only our weaknesses and sins that are uncovered in our conversations with God. The more we communicate with Him, the more we learn about Him. God has always been a self-revealing God;

otherwise we could know nothing about Him. Undoubtedly, the best course on theology (the study of God) is time spent in prayer. When we are in His presence, He can illuminate His Word to us as no seminary professor ever could. Jesus is still the great Teacher, and the Spirit of Christ dwells in the believer to "take of what is Mine [Jesus'] and declare it to you. All things that the Father has are Mine. Therefore I said that He will take of Mine and declare it to you" (John 16:14*b*,15).

Prayer Seeks to Influence God

It would be both foolish and dishonest for us to pretend that all of our praying is merely to seek an audience with God in order to have a conversation with Him. The naked truth is that we are endeavoring to influence Him. We have been taught that our asking is the thing that influences God to function on our behalf. Some say that prayer does influence Him, while many others declare that it does not influence Him. Both are correct. Prayer does not influence God's purpose, but prayer does influence His actions. God has already purposed to do every right thing that has ever been prayed for, but He does nothing without our consent. Our lack of willingness often hinders Him in working His purposes in us. When we learn His purposes and make them our prayers, we give Him the opportunity to act.

This is why prayer is so vital. When we call to God and ask of Him, we have already turned our faces toward Him. Our wills have acted doubly—in turning from our way and in turning to Him for His help. Our calling to God is the point of sympathetic contact with Him, where our purposes become the same as His purposes. If we pray in the Spirit, we ask for what He purposes to do, and we discover that purpose.

In the Sermon on the Mount, Jesus said, "Your Father knows the things you have need of before you ask Him" (Matthew 6:8), and the very next line starts the Lord's Prayer. If the Father knows what we need, why pray? Because we do not know what we need or what the Father has purposed to give. Our praying will influence God to reveal His purposes, and when we pray for this revelation, He is influenced to release it to us. Here, again, the Holy Spirit is a great assistant to our praying. "Likewise the Spirit also helps in our weaknesses. For we do not know what we should pray for as we ought, but the Spirit Himself makes intercession for us with groanings which cannot be uttered. Now He who searches the hearts knows what the mind of the Spirit is, because He makes intercession for the saints according to the will of God" (Romans 8:26,27).

Prayer's Purpose Is to Get an Answer From God

It has long and properly been said that if prayer is asking, answered prayer is receiving. Prayer is a two-way communication. If we do not hear from God, we have cut the prayer time too short; we've "said our piece" and hung up. However, we should not stop praying just because we are certain that God has heard us. We should maintain the conversation until God answers, for the prayer cycle starts at gaining an audience with God and proceeds to gaining an answer from God. The Bible promise is not that if we would call, God would listen. It is, "Call to Me, and I will *answer* you" (Jeremiah 33:3, italics added).

Receiving an answer from God is not necessarily synonymous with getting our own way. God is not a dispensing machine that must always deliver the merchandise requested when the coin of faith is inserted. He is an all-wise heavenly Father who desires the best for our lives and who knows that we do not understand what is best for ourselves. He will answer us unfailingly, but He will not indulge us consistently. His love is too great toward us. Would a loving father give a sharp knife to a baby for a toy?

> We pray for escape from our trial, but He gives us grace to endure it; we pray for release from our burden, but He gives us strength to bear it.

God will invariably answer prayer, but He answers it in His own way. We pray for deliverance from Satan, and God gives us power over Satan. We pray for escape from our trial, but He gives us grace to endure it; we pray for release from our burden, but He gives us strength to bear it. God doesn't take orders, but He does take notice of our needs.

God's answer to prayer may come in one of three forms. Sometimes God says *yes*. That is what we expect to hear, for we always pray anticipating a positive answer. When we get a *yes*, we respond in thanksgiving. At other times, God gives a clear *no*. This is a definite answer which often precipitates a spiritual tantrum. Often God's answer is *later*. The petition has been granted, but God has put it on "hold" until we mature sufficiently to participate safely in that answer. This form of answer is often very confusing to us, for we do not know how long "later" is.

If prayer's purpose is to get an answer from God, then we should pray expecting an answer. There is no room for vagueness in our praying. If we have a petition, it should be stated clearly, right to the point, and given in an expectant tone. Far too many prayers give God great loopholes as a "cover-up" if there seems to be no answer. I have listened to a great many prayers that would require divine revelation for anyone to know if they were ever answered. These same persons would never be so vague in dealing with a banker.

We need to remind ourselves that we have an audience before the King of kings and Lord of lords. Whining and begging have no place in His presence. He has received us into His presence, and He has invited us to state our desires. Our behavior should be in harmony with this great privilege. We have no basis for pride when in God's presence, but God is not pleased with self-negation and false humility either. When we respond to His invitation to "be anxious for nothing, but in everything by prayer and supplication, with thanksgiving, let your requests be made known to God" (Philippians 4:6), we need to make our petitions with dignity. Neither brashness nor bashfulness is in order. We should be like the child responding to a father who has offered a choice of ice cream flavors. Request what you want with a smile. Speak up with rejoicing in your voice. The answer has been promised; we are merely declaring our choice.

Prayer Becomes a Channel for God's Answer

If the sole purpose of prayer were to get an answer, it would not matter who did the praying. In American Christianity, this seems to be a prevailing attitude. We call prayer towers or write to radio and television evangelists asking that their "prayer partners" intercede for us. This is profitable if the request is for others to pray with us, but it can be highly dangerous if we desire them to pray for or instead of us, for **the very act of prayer prepares us to receive God's answer.**

This principle is seen in the life of the prophet Jeremiah. Repeatedly, kings and leaders requested him to seek an answer from God on their behalf, and, just as repeatedly, the answer from God was refused. The classic example follows God's fulfillment of Jeremiah's repeated prophecy of Judah's captivity by Babylon. The leaders of the small remnant that was left in the land "said to Jeremiah the prophet, 'Please let our petition be acceptable to you, and pray for us to the Lord your God, for all this remnant...that the Lord your God may show us the way in which we should walk and the thing we should do'" (Jeremiah 42:2,3).

Jeremiah was given a pledge that "whether it is pleasing or displeasing, we will obey the voice of the Lord our God to whom we send you, that it may be well with us when we obey the voice of the Lord our God" (Jeremiah 42:6).

For ten days, Jeremiah sought the face of the Lord in prayer, and then God gave him the requested message. When Jeremiah reported God's word to these leaders,

> Part of the process of answered prayer is asked prayer. Our asking prepares us for receiving.

they refused it, declared that it could not be a word from God. They completely disobeyed everything that God had said. This is what Jeremiah had expected. This kind of thing had happened before. During his lifetime, Jeremiah had been thrown into a pit of mire, locked in prison, and kept under house arrest; he was about to be forced to go to Egypt, where tradition says, he was murdered. All this adverse treatment was for simply declaring what God said to those who had asked Jeremiah to intercede before God on their behalf.

Those who will not pray but desire others to pray for them are unprepared for the kind of answers God gives. Part of the process of answered prayer is asked prayer. Our asking prepares us for receiving. As Jeremiah spent ten days praying, he was also preparing his heart spiritually to accept God's answer. When this answer was given to nonpraying, carnally minded people, they rebelled against it.

This didn't end in Jeremiah's day. Accepting God's answer to our prayer is often difficult, especially when God doesn't tell us what we want to hear. Sheila, a Christian girl, was infatuated with the drummer of a Christian musical group. When he asked her to marry him, she said she wanted to pray about it. She presented her petition to the church during a prayer session; and she, with the other Christians, prayed earnestly for direction from God. Several words were given that declared that this was not God's will for her life. Additionally, God mercifully allowed her to see moral failure in this young man during the next week. At the next prayer meeting, she thanked the saints for their prayers and said it was very obvious to her that God didn't want her to marry this man.

The next thing we heard was that she had secretly married him and, subsequently, bore his child. He was more persuasive than God in her life at that season. She reaped bitter fruit out of this decision, for her husband spent years in jail for income tax evasion, and the marriage eventually ended in divorce. None of us is compelled to accept God's answer to our prayers, but if we don't, we'll bear the bitter fruit of having our own way.

The submission and surrender that prayer requires automatically prepares us to surrender to God's will when the answer is given. Writing to another to pray for us or calling our pastor, requesting that the local congregation pray for us and our needs, may seem like an easy short-cut to contacting God. Even if these people succeed in "praying through" for us, it is most unlikely that we will be ready spiritually to receive and respond to the answer from God. It is somewhat like a human helping a baby chick get out of its egg. The chick may escape its prison, but it will die; for the exercise of pecking a hole in the shell is necessary for it to live outside of that shell.

It is not enough that there be a prayer channel that allows us to contact God. It is imperative that the needy person be a prayer channel that contacts God if the answer is to be life-changing. The prayer life of a man's wife cannot substitute for his personal contact with God, nor will the prayer in a local congregation ever successfully supplant the prayer of individuals.

Jesus said, "Whatever you ask the Father in My name He may give you" (John 15:16). The asking makes it possible for the Father to give to you. God is Spirit, and He must be contacted in spirit. Equally, He must contact us in the realm of our spirit. As Paul put it, "The Spirit Himself bears witness with our spirit that we are children of God" (Romans 8:16). God's communication is from Spirit to spirit. Prayer ascends as a channel of communication between our spirits and God's Spirit. Until we pray, then, God does not have the desired channel through which to communicate an answer. Little wonder, then, that James says, "You do not have because you do not ask" (James 4:2*b*).

Prayer Is a Process of Enlargement

God's promise through Jeremiah was far more than merely answered prayer. He said, "Call to Me, and I will answer you, and *show you great and mighty things*, which you do not know" (Jeremiah 33:3, italics added). Praying people are seeing people, for the praying person's vision is not restricted to his or her narrow confines; the vision becomes world-wide. When we pray, our vision is released beyond the boundaries of the physical and emotional world, and we see things in the spirit world. Prayer offers us a panoramic view from the top—a chance to see things as God sees them. Problems that seemed insoluble are seen in a new light. Perplexing circumstances seem very normal. Even our own lives are considered from a different angle when we pray.

Every time we see from God's perspective, our sight is enlarged. He has promised to show us "great and mighty things." The greater our spiritual vision, the more lofty our spiritual life. Most of us spend our lives occupied with puny, insignificant things; majoring in minors. Prayer gives us a chance at "great and mighty things." It lifts us out of the mundane. It frees us from being earthbound and gives us the wings of eagles to soar into God's greatness, ascending to His glorious presence.

God gives us opportunities to practice focusing on Him in the midst of trials. I particularly found this to be the case in the following instance: The story wasn't even close to being true. Whether it was a malicious lie or just exaggerated misinformation, I did not know. I only knew that what was being said cast a shadow on my character, and it hurt. I set my heart to earnest prayer while pleading with God to stop the mouths of these persons and to justify me before my congregation.

As I prayed, I became gloriously aware of the presence of the Lord. I was reminded of the false accusations He faced and how victoriously He fulfilled His mission in spite of them. The glory of the eternal heavens filled my soul so completely that my earthbound, tarnished reputation didn't seem important at all.

God's answer to my prayer was not to close the mouths of the slanderers, but to open my spiritual eyes to the glory that awaited me. God didn't justify me in the eyes of my congregation, but he justified me in His eyes, which is far greater.

It is one thing to be told to "think big" and to "attempt great things," but to be able to grasp things of greatness is something else. The "great things" of God's Word and the "mighty things" of God's Spirit are revealed and given to the praying person. Prayer is the channel to greatness of being and mightiness of action.

Prayer has enlarged me more than anything else in life. My vision for ministry has come through the prayer channel, and the power to implement that vision has also come during time spent in God's presence. God enlarges His work in and through us when we offer Him a consistent prayer channel.

There is also revelation in prayer, for God promises to show us things "which you do not know." Daniel was in prayer each time a revelation was given to him. Paul speaks of being in prayer when revelation was given, and John was in prayer on the Isle of Patmos when the great Revelation of Jesus Christ was given to him. God reveals His will, His word, His work, and His ways through the prayer channel. He reveals our self, our sin, our stubbornness, and our self-righteousness through prayer. Furthermore, God reveals His provision in the past, His plan for the present, and His purpose for the future when we are in communication with Him in prayer.

Receiving a new vision, an enlargement, or a revelation from God is far less a mystery and more the results of the discipline of prayer. When the channel is open, insight and revelation can flow. When this enlargement is effected in us, we can be available to God for the ministry of intercession, for prayer is the God-given channel for intercession.

For Reflection

1. If your prayer is a channel for communication, with whom are you communicating?
2. Do you think that prayer influences God?
3. When you pray, do you expect to get an answer from God? Really?
4. Could prayer be a channel through which God gets to us? How?

rayer Ascends As the Channel for Intercession

When Paul wrote to his "true son in the faith" (1 Timothy 1:2), he said, "I exhort first of all that supplications, prayers, intercessions, and giving of thanks be made for all men" (1 Timothy 2:1). It is the only place in the New Testament where all four words for prayer are found linked together. It may be that Paul was not seeking to make strong distinctions between these terms as much as he was trying to cover all forms of prayer in his injunction to this young pastor.

Nevertheless, it does seem that the four Greek words that Paul used are arranged in an ascending order. The word *supplications* comes from the Greek *deesis,* which basically means "petition." It gives prominence to the expression of one's own personal need. The word *prayer* is a translation of *proseuche,* which is used only for prayer to God, and suggests the element of devotion. It is the most general word for prayer in the New Testament, and it is used thirty-seven times. The word *intercessions,* in this verse, comes from the Greek word *enteuxis* and is used only in 1 Timothy. We commonly think of intercession as mediation: taking the place of another. In a very strict sense Christ is the only true mediator between God and persons (see 1 Timothy 2:5); yet we read of Paul's prayers on behalf of the churches, and he urges us to "bear one another's burdens, and so fulfill the law of Christ" (Galatians 6:2). Paul's fourth word for prayer is *eucharistia* or *the giving of thanks.* It is the grateful acknowledgment of past mercies, as distinguished from the earnest seeking of future gifts.

Having already spoken of supplications and prayer, which would certainly cover all forms of petition for oneself, Paul must have had a good reason for placing the familiar word *intercessions* so high on his list. What situation could necessitate

71

coming into the presence of an all-knowing God in an intimate, personal way to lay before Him a need or burden which is not really one's own?

The Underlying Situation

We need to remember that we humans are God's wayward children, like the prodigal son. Made in His image and given life from His breath, humanity departed from God. God needs persons for the implementation of His plan of redemption, for His plan of bringing wayward children back to Himself. God Himself became human for the greatest step in His great "recovery act."

Let's look back through history at seven facts that give us a background and explain why intercessory prayer is so vital:

1. "The earth is the Lord's, and all its fullness" (Psalm 24:1*a*). By virtue of creation, the earth is God's.

2. God, however, gave the dominion of the earth to mankind. David asked, "What is man that You are mindful of him, and the son of man that You visit him?... You have made him to have dominion over the works of Your hands; You have put all things under his feet" (Psalm 8:4,6).

3. In trust from God, man held the dominion of the earth, but he transferred this dominion to someone else, being deceived into doing so. It was an act of disobedience to God and of obedience to the devil.

4. This means that the effective dominion over this world-system is neither God's nor mankind's. Adam and Eve transferred it to Satan. Jesus acknowledged this in repeatedly calling Satan "the ruler of this world" (See John 12:31; 14:30; 16:11). While it is not Satan's world, he is acting as the usurper prince or governor.

5. God has been eager to swing the world back to its original dominion for His own sake, for mankind's sake, and for the earth's sake. To do so, He needs persons, the progeny of the original trustees (Adam and Eve), through whom He can return this earth to its first allegiance. Since man forfeited the dominion over the earth, he must regain it. This is why the perfect God-man was incarnated; Jesus

came to earth to head a movement to bring the world back to its first allegiance.

6. The usurper prince and God's man had a combat over this dominion. From the cruel, malicious cradle attack on the babies of Bethlehem until Calvary's inhuman crucifixion, it continued. The master-prince of this world fought his best, and his worst, through Jesus' Nazareth years, then into the wilderness and Gethsemane and, finally, at Calvary. The Scripture unequivocally records that the God-man was the victor. On the third day after the crucifixion, the bars of death were snapped like rotting wood, and Jesus rose as the victor over all the powers and pseudo-authorities of the enemy. Both heaven and hell knew that Satan was completely defeated.

7. The seventh factor that underlies the need for intercessory prayer has at least four contributing elements to it:
   a. Satan refuses to acknowledge his defeat,
   b. He refuses to surrender his dominion until he is forced to do so.
   c. He is supported in his ambitions by sinful and selfish mankind; he has mankind's consent to his control.
   d. Satan still hopes to make his possession of the earth permanent. His desire to overthrow God, as pictured in Isaiah 14, is still paramount in his mind.

At this moment, it appears that Satan is trying hard to get a "jesus," that is, a man—a descendant of the original trustees to whom the dominion of the world was entrusted—to stand for him even as Jesus stood for God. This "Antichrist" will personify Satan just as Jesus was the personification of God. When Satan succeeds in this, the last desperate crisis will come, and Christ Jesus will return to finalize His victory.

We seem to be near this event, but it is not yet upon us. Until then, prayer is the channel through which God regains control of His wayward creations. Prayer, therefore, is basically a person (an original trustee), with his or her life in full touch with the victor and completely out of touch with the pretender-prince, living on the earth (over which Satan has usurped authority) and insistently claiming that Satan shall yield, step-by-step and life-by-life, before Christ's victory.

Jesus is the conqueror, and Satan is the conquered. This defeated devil must yield before Christ's advance, and he must also yield before the man or woman who stands for Jesus. Reluctantly, angrily, and as slowly as he can, he will yield. His clutches will loosen, and he will flee before the God-man, Christ Jesus. But God needs a protesting person on earth through whom He may enforce the claims of Christ against this prince. This forms the fundamental basis for intercessory prayer.

An Interceding Priest

By God's merciful grace, this intercession does not begin with us. We are told, "Therefore He is also able to save to the uttermost those who come to God through Him, since He always lives to make intercession for them. For such a High Priest was fitting for us..." (Hebrews 7:25,26*a*).

When Adam submitted to the trickery of the devil and exercised his will against the known will of God, he immediately became aware of a change in his relationship with God. Guilt, fear, and self-condemnation caused him to try to hide himself from God. Sin has always caused people to run from God instead of to Him; they do not understand that there is a mediator who on their behalf will stand before the divine being.

David understood the difficulty of fleeing from God's presence, for he wrote, "Where can I go from Your Spirit? Or where can I flee from Your presence? If I ascend into heaven, You are there; if I make my bed in hell, behold, You are there. If I take the wings of the morning, and dwell in the uttermost parts of the sea, even there Your hand shall lead me" (Psalms 139:7-10*a*). Where can sinful, guilty persons go to get away from God? It has wisely been said, "The only place we can hide from God's presence is in His presence."

This is illustrated in the lives of the Hebrew slaves in Egypt. Because of the mediatorial work of Moses, they were spared the most severe plagues God sent upon the Egyptians. Their land of Goshen became a haven of God's presence in the shadow of death.

From that day onward, everything God did with them was an attempt to bring them into a more intimate relationship with Himself. He instituted a sacrificial system for the handling of sin which included a priesthood that represented the people before God, and God before the people.

The high priest was chosen especially to be the intercessor for the people. Annually, he entered the holy of holies. With a basin of blood in one hand and a censer of incense in the other, he made atonement for the people. If his offering was received, the people knew that the intercession of their high priest had been accepted and that their sins were forgiven.

Jesus is declared repeatedly to be our high priest. His special duty is to represent us before God in the matter of our sins. He became one of us in order to represent us fully

> Christ's very presence at the right hand of God is an eternal act of intercession on mankind's behalf.

to God, yet because He never ceased being God, He can represent God to us. His reconciling work was completed once and for all on the cross. Unlike the Old Testament high priests who had to repeat the pattern of sacrifices, "this Man, after He had offered one sacrifice for sins forever, sat down at the right hand of God...for by one offering He has perfected forever those who are being sanctified" (Hebrews 10:12,14).

Christ's very presence at the right hand of God is an eternal act of intercession on mankind's behalf. John said, "My little children, these things I write to you, so that you may not sin. And if anyone sins, we have an Advocate with the Father, Jesus Christ the righteous" (1 John 2:1). Paul wrote similarly in his letter to the church at Rome. He asked, "Who is he who condemns? It is Christ who died, and furthermore is also risen, who is even at the right hand of God, who also makes intercession for us" (Romans 8:34).

It is not that Jesus is praying to the Father, asking the Father to forgive us for our sins; Jesus and the Father are one, and they worked as one in the whole scheme of redemption. "God was in Christ reconciling the world to Himself" (2 Corinthians 5:19*a*). Surely, Jesus would not have to plead with the Father to do what He had purposed, planned, and paid such an enormous price to accomplish.

The intercession of Jesus is unlike the intercession of the Old Testament prophets and priests who prayed earnestly on behalf of a sinning people. They sought to change God's mind about punishing a disobedient race. In contrast to this, the intercession of Jesus is a blood-stained intercession. He did not ask the Father to forgive until the full penalty for sin had been paid at Calvary. That ultimate penalty, we know, was death. "As it is appointed for men to die once, but after this the judgment, so Christ was offered once to bear the sins of many. To those who eagerly wait for Him, He will appear a second time, apart from sin, for salvation" (Hebrews 9:27,28). The basis of Christ's intercession, then, is His vicarious, atoning work at Calvary. He need not plead God's mercy, nor must He plead our great need. He merely points to His finished work and says, "It is covered. It is paid in full."

In a broad sense, we could say that an officer of the law assigned to guard a person whose life is in danger is an intercessor. The officer's very presence stands between the threatened and the one who threatens. Similarly, Christ's person and what He stands for make Him our intercessor in heaven. His very office mediates between God and mankind.

If our enemy tries to interfere with our relational standing with God, he will encounter the superior force of Christ Jesus; on the other hand, our sins cannot become a distressing force against a holy God, because they get no further than the redemptive work of Jesus Christ. Both God and man benefit by this intercession of Jesus.

The intercession of Christ Jesus is unlike not only the intercession of the Old Testament priests; it is unlike any intercession ever seen here upon this earth. No person can plead successfully with God to overlook sin, but Jesus has provided a way for God to forgive and cleanse that sin. We may earnestly intercede and implore God to extend grace and mercy to people, but Jesus is the very source of God's grace and mercy to mankind. Ours is always the intercession of petition, while *the intercession of Jesus is one of provision.*

The intercession of our high priest, Christ Jesus, is from above us, and it is vicarious. He intercedes for our inabilities. What we cannot do, He has done.

An Interceding *Paraclete*

In contrast to this work of Christ Jesus is the interceding work of the Holy Spirit, the blessed *Paraclete* or "Helper" that Jesus promised to send after His ascension. While the intercession of Jesus is entirely for us, the work of the Spirit is with us. Jesus intercedes from above us, but the Holy Spirit intercedes from within us. Jesus intercedes for our inabilities, while the Holy Spirit pleads for our ignorance, for we don't even know how we should pray. Having faced this dilemma, Paul wrote, "Now He who searches the hearts knows what the mind of the Spirit is, because He makes intercession for the saints according to the will of God" (Romans 8:27).

One of the vivid signs of the indwelling Spirit of God is the deep sense of dissatisfaction that believers experience. Like a kidnapped hostage who longs fearfully for home, the Christian knows deep heart groanings after God. We were made for God, and nothing but God can satisfy the heart. More than just that, while the Spirit within pleads the sonship of us believers, our earthly environment is filled with painful contradictions to this high calling; it forces lengthy separations from the conscious awareness of God's presence. Having tasted the life that is to come, the Spirit-filled Christian can hardly get comfortable with this life.

This upward pull toward "home" is difficult to put into words. At times when I bow in prayer and express deep gratitude for God's abundant provisions, I'm actually ashamed at the sense of dissatisfaction I feel. Though we don't know how to express it, the Holy Spirit does. He can wondrously thank God for present provision while crying out for more and higher provisions, found only in the divine presence. The prayer we do not know how to pray is prayed through us by the Spirit. Often it is inarticulate (unintelligible) prayer that successfully bypasses the censorship of our conscious mind and releases the cryings of our spirit. This must be what Paul referred to when he said, "…I will pray with the spirit, and I will also pray with the understanding…" (1 Corinthians 14:15).

On repeated occasions, my lips have expressed to God the thoughts of my conscious mind, but at the same time my spirit has ached, groaned, and travailed for something that my mind could not grasp. The inner cry overcame the conscious prayer, yet I could not formulate thoughts or speak words that expressed what I was feeling. At such times a Helper beyond myself has interceded for me. Sometimes He has prayed within me off and on for days, until I found an inner release. Subsequently, there would come a dramatic change in the direction of my ministry. God had to change me in order to change what He could do through me, but I did not understand the mind of God; so the Holy Spirit prayed on my behalf without the need of conscious thought. God, who knows the mind of His Spirit, answered according to His own perfect will.

This inner groaning, this intercession of the Spirit that is too big for utterance, is a powerful plea with God. Those who give themselves to prayer soon learn that they do not know how to pray, but, with the advocacy of Christ above them and the intercession of the Holy Spirit within them, they discover that they frequently need be little more than a participant with the great Teacher who assists their feeble efforts.

When Paul wrote, "Likewise the Spirit also helps in our weaknesses. For we do not know what we should pray for as we ought, but the Spirit Himself makes intercession for us with groanings which cannot be uttered" (Romans 8:26), he used the Greek word *sunantilambano*. We translate it *helps*. It is really three words put together: *sun*, "together with"; *anti*, "over against"; and *lambano*, "to take." The combined word speaks of a person coming to another's aid by taking hold of the load he is carrying and helping to ease the burden; he does not take the entire load, but he helps carry it.

> Our praying will never be replaced by the Spirit, but it can be restructured by Him.

This Greek word is also used where Martha complained about Mary to the Lord Jesus by saying, "Tell her to help me"

78

(Luke 10:40). Martha was pleading with Mary for a "helping hand." Similarly, the Holy Spirit, who lives within the believer, comes to help in spiritual problems and difficulties, not by taking over the responsibility and giving the Christian an automatic deliverance, but by lending a helping hand. Our praying will never be replaced by the Spirit, but it can be restructured by Him; for He knows both what is in the depths of our hearts and what is the mind of God.

The weaknesses Paul refers to clearly include our inability to know what to pray for. We know what the general objects of prayer are, but we do not know what the specific, detailed objects of prayer are in any given emergency or situation. In the Greek, the definite article is used before the word *what.* Paul declares literally, "We do not know the what we should pray for, the particular what." We generally know the end and pray toward that, but we may not know what is necessary in order for us to attain this end. The Holy Spirit overcomes this ignorance by praying through us.

Paul continues, saying that "the Spirit Himself makes intercession." Here he uses the Greek word *huperentugchano,* which is a word of rescue by one who "happens on" another who is in trouble. *Thayer's Greek Lexicon* states, "Although we have no very definite conception of what we desire, and cannot state it in fit language (as we ought) in our prayer but only disclose it by inarticulate groanings, yet God receives these groanings as acceptable prayer inasmuch as they come from a soul full of the Holy Spirit." Nineteenth-century English scholar Henry Alford said, "The Holy Spirit of God dwelling in us, knowing our wants better than we, Himself pleads in our prayers, raising us to higher and holier desires than we can express in words, which can only find utterance in sighings and aspirations."

Although the indwelling Spirit is distinct from our human spirit, He is in such an intimate relationship with it that He is able to interpret to God our spirit's most inarticulate longings. Prayer is no mere human activity. God Himself intercedes for us in heaven, and He prays through us on earth. Even when we do not know for what or how to pray, our human deficiency is supplemented by divine power as the Holy Spirit takes up the heavy end of our prayer burden and prays it through with us, "according to the will of God" (Romans 8:27).

In speaking on this passage, Charles H. Spurgeon said: "Groanings which cannot be uttered are often prayers which cannot be refused." Such prayers are so inspired by the Holy Spirit that they are harmonious with the perfect will of God and true to the need of the one praying. Of course, they cannot be refused!

Beyond question, one of the important ministries of the Spirit is that of aiding us in prayer. Aiding—not replacing.

An Interceding Person

E.M. Bounds, in his book *The Weapon of Prayer*, wrote: "What the church needs today is not more or better machinery, nor new organizations or more and novel methods, but men whom the Holy Ghost can use—men of prayer, men mighty in prayer. The Holy Ghost does not flow through methods, but through men. He does not come on machinery, but on men. He does not anoint plans, but men—men of prayer." If that was true in his generation, it must be even more true of our materialistic society. Modern theologians argue whether or not God actually answers prayer, but the Bible is predominantly a book of prayer. Someone traced 667 prayers for specific things in the Bible and found 454 traceable, recorded answers to those prayers—that means nearly seventy percent. That should settle the question of whether or not God answers prayer!

When Jesus taught His disciples to pray, it was clear that their emphasis was to be on others. His prayer began with the plural term "our." Jesus did not teach us to pray to my Father, but our Father! Later in the prayer, Jesus uses such statements as "give us," "lead us" and "forgive us" (see Matthew 6:9-13). When we pray for others, we do not stand with outstretched hands hoping to receive something for ourselves. We stand at God's side, working together with Him, in the pleading for God's perfect will in the lives of others. We pray that what He has graciously done in us also will be done in the lives of those for whom we pray.

None of us will ever be able to intercede like Jesus, nor will we ever be able to match the true need with the perfect will of God, as the Holy Spirit does. But intercession of Christians is God's method for involving His followers more completely in the totality of His plan. The intercession of Jesus is from above us, that of the Spirit is within us, but personal intercession is through us. It completes the triangle of prayer.

Paul told the churches regularly that he prayed for them daily, and he asked that the saints pray earnestly for him and for the ministry that God had entrusted to him. This was not lack of faith on the part of Paul; it was his active involvement in what God was doing and an invitation to others to do likewise.

People will never know the excitement I feel and the sense of relief I receive when they tell me that they have been praying earnestly for me. The ministry that God has entrusted to me is far bigger than I am, and there are satanic oppositions and fleshly weaknesses that could destroy the effectiveness of the message of worship. I could rightfully fear the outcome if I had to stand alone, but God, through His Spirit, burdens others to take me before the throne of grace for strength, guidance, and anointing.

The story is told of a young English pastor who proved to be a grave disappointment to his congregation. Criticism was rampant when a few older women in the church determined to pray for him. Every time this man entered the pulpit, a small committee of "prayer warriors" interceded for him in the prayer room directly under the platform. Need I tell you that this young man became one of the leading voices for Christianity in his lifetime?

In ways that we do not understand, God seems to intervene in our affairs only in response to our petitions. Sometimes when

> I could rightfully fear the outcome if I had to stand alone.

one of us has failed to pray according to His will or when the enemy comes against one of us with great strength, the Holy Spirit moves upon another believer, or several, to intercede for that person in prayer. At times, this becomes a life-and-death matter.

When I was much younger, I led a congregation in the

construction of a new church facility. Since we were building with all donated labor, I was acting as both contractor and supervisor of construction. Just as we were preparing to shingle the roof of the auditorium, a light snow fell, and ice became a problem. We were afraid we might lose the sheeting, but that ice just wouldn't melt.

On Saturday, as a crew of volunteers waited for the roof to clear, I crawled impatiently through the steeple hole onto the top of the roof. I wanted to see if it was safe. Well, I lost my balance on the ice and started sliding headfirst down that high roof directly toward a pile of bricks on the ground. There was nothing to grab, and the men screamed in fear as they saw me pick up speed as if I were on a toboggan. Just as my head came over the edge of the roof, I stopped my descent as though I had hit something. It was not a gradual slowing down—it was sudden. To the amazement of all of us, I was able to turn myself around with my head facing the peak of the roof. I then slid uphill and back to the spot where my descent had begun. Shaking, I crawled off the roof fully aware that I had experienced "a close call."

It was not until after the services on Sunday that I understood what had happened. A member of my congregation had been washing dishes at that very time, and the Spirit within her commanded her to pray. With dripping hands she ran into her bedroom, dropped down on her knees, and prayed in the Spirit. When the spirit of intercession lifted, she asked the Lord what she had been praying for. In a vision, He showed her my slide down the roof, and she saw the hand of God stop me at the edge and push me back to the ridge. What if she had failed to respond to the Spirit's plea to pray? I have always felt that Sister Connie Smith will have a share in whatever rewards are given for the ministries that have come through me since that day.

There are times when the Holy Spirit urges us to be a channel through whom He can intercede for a specific need in the body of Christ. He may pray through us for nations we have never visited and for people totally unknown to us. We may never understand why we felt such a burden of prayer, but the Spirit directs us and controls that praying according to the will of God.

There are times when we are fully aware of the need for which we are praying. In the midst of our praying, we find ourselves taking that person's place and praying as though the need were ours.

Church history records that John Knox prayed—and Queen Mary trembled. She is reported to have declared that she feared his prayers more than she feared all the armies of Europe. Surely Satan, too, trembles when the weakest saint gets on his or her knees to intercede for others. The power is not in the person but in the anointed prayer that will flow from the heart.

John of Cronstadt, a nineteenth-century Russian priest, said, "Why has our sincere prayer for each other such great power over others? Because of the fact that by cleaving to God during prayer I become one spirit with Him, and unite with myself by faith, and love, those for whom I pray; for the Holy Ghost acting in me also acts at the same time in them, for He accomplishes all things."

That God has chosen to honor the prayers of one for another is illustrated amply in the Scriptures. To Abimelech, God said of Abraham, "He will pray for you and you shall live" (Genesis 20:7). When God expressed His anger with the comforters of Job, He told them, "My servant Job shall pray for you. For I will accept him, lest I deal with you according to your folly…" (Job 42:8b).

An interesting by-product of intercessory prayer is the change of attitude it produces in the one who prays. In his book *A Serious Call to a Devout and Holy Life*, William Law wrote: "There is nothing that makes us love a man so much as praying for him." All intercessors can say a loud "Amen!"

An Interceding Pair

Jesus both taught and exemplified plural ministries. When He sent His disciples out in ministry, He always sent them in pairs. From this we might expect that He should suggest that intercession would best be done by persons joined together by the Spirit. He told His disciples, "I say to you that if two of you agree on earth concerning anything that they ask, it will be done for them by My Father in heaven" (Matthew 18:19). The

83

agreement certainly must go beyond mental acknowledgment. It is a case of the same Spirit praying for the same thing through two or more persons.

All who have given themselves to prayer have learned the value of having a prayer partner—someone who will agree with them in prayer and through whom the Spirit may pray harmoniously. Jesus said that, if we are united with someone else in our intercessory prayers, what we ask will be done by God the Father.

Some years ago, I was pulled away from my word processor by an insistent, ringing phone. It was a pastor friend of mine in another city, whose church my daughter attended. "Judson," he began, "are you sitting down?"

"No," I said.

"Then please sit down," he continued. "I'm afraid I have some very bad news for you. Your daughter was found unconscious in her bedroom this morning. She is in the hospital—barely alive on support systems. The doctors have been working with her all morning, but there is no visible sign of improvement. I had planned to wait until there was a more definite word to give to you, but my wife urged me to call now so that you could go to prayer."

I thanked him for the hours he had spent at the hospital and for calling me. After I hung up the phone, I felt numb all over. I stepped out into the hallway just as the classes of the Bible school were changing. Elbowing my way through the students, I made it to the little prayer room. Just as I stepped in, two of the teachers walked by. Taking them by their arms, I pulled them into the prayer room and told them about my phone call.

"Please pray with me," I requested.

"How shall we pray?" they responded.

"I don't know," I said. "Let's ask the Holy Spirit to pray through us."

Almost immediately, I heard myself praying, "Not my will, but Thine be done." Over and over again that prayer came out of my lips, and it seemed to come from deep within me. The teachers joined me in this prayer. It seemed as if God Himself were in that little room praying with us.

Our prayers were interrupted by the bells signaling the start of another class session.

"We'll stay here with you," the teachers said.

"That won't be necessary," I replied. "The Spirit has prayed through us. Now it is time to trust God."

I went back to my office and heard the phone ring. That same pastor was on the line, and he said, "I certainly wish I had the contact with God that you seem to have. By the time I got back to your daughter, she had regained consciousness. She was trying to get out of bed and has assured us that everything is all right."

The doctors had warned of severe complications if she survived the ordeal, but they were wrong. In that brief period of time, God restored my daughter's health completely, and she is now very active in the medical profession.

"If two of you shall agree...it will be done." Knowing that, James says that we should "pray for one another," adding, "The effective, fervent prayer of a righteous man avails much" (James 5:16*b*). Then he recounts the story of Elijah's powerful intercession that closed and later opened the heavens. What power God has invested in united intercession. Two persons praying the same prayers anywhere on earth will always raise a commotion in heaven. Little wonder, then, that we are challenged to "bear one another's burdens, and so fulfill the law of Christ" (Galatians 6:2). Lifting the heavy load that another is carrying is the very heart of intercession—of the Spirit and of the saints.

There is interceding prayer above us, through us and, in the case of an interceding pair, among us. From every possible direction prayer ascends to glory as an offering. What chance does the enemy have for success? "What then shall we say to these things? If God is for us, who can be against us?" (Romans 8:31).

Intercessory prayer, in its varied forms, deals with people, problems and spiritual powers. The prayer of faith, however, deals more exclusively with God. It is learning to say, with authority, what God has said.

For Reflection

1. What is it generally called when we feel impressed to pray for someone else?
2. Do we have any authority for declaring Jesus to be our intercessor?
3. How does the Holy Spirit intercede on our behalf? On Christ's behalf?
4. What part do we play in His intercession?

rayer Ascends As the Channel for the Release of Faith

That prayer demands faith is obvious. The Bible declares, "But without faith it is impossible to please Him, for he who comes to God must believe that He is, and that He is a rewarder of those who diligently seek Him" (Hebrews 11:6). The very act of praying evidences a firm conviction that there is a God who is approachable and who can be entreated on our behalf. This level of faith probably will not move mountains, but it will move persons from self-dependence to crying out to God.

Paul declared that "God has dealt to each one a measure of faith" (Romans 12:3), but elsewhere says that "not all have faith" (2 Thessalonians 3:2). Paul speaks of erring from the faith (see 1 Timothy 6:10), overthrowing the faith (see 2 Timothy 2:18), and departing from the faith (see 1 Timothy 4:1).

It would seem, then, that God's initial impartation of a firm conviction in His existence and availability can be lost through disuse, misuse, or abuse. Since faith comes from God to humanity it must be a renewable resource. Furthermore, it is a divine energy that must be renewed. Faith, like electricity, does not store well. It goes from the source to the need quickly, but it is expended in meeting that need. The New Testament position on faith is that we receive it when God speaks, and we release it in saying what God has spoken. In a very real sense we are the channels of faith, but we are never the creators of it.

Prayer Provides for Receiving Faith

When Christ taught His disciples about prayer in the Sermon on the Mount, the emphasis was upon speaking to God,

87

but when He taught them about prayer enroute to the Garden of Gethsemane, His emphasis was on hearing God. The first teaching was based upon "When you pray, say…" (Luke 11:2), while the final instruction centered around, "These things I have spoken to you while being present with you. But the Helper, the Holy Spirit, whom the Father will send in My name, He will teach you all things, and bring to your remembrance all things that I said to you" (John 14:25,26). The beginning levels of prayer are very self-centered and often express little more than the needs and desires of the petitioner. It is the longing expression from the all-needy to the Almighty. This is not wrong—it is even commanded—but it is primitive. As our ministry in prayer matures, it becomes a channel through which we receive faith that will enable us to pray the will and wants of God rather than merely plead our own yearnings.

The word *faith* is very common to the English language: In the secular context, its definition is "believing the word of another." But Biblical faith is a little more complicated than that. Biblical faith is not a mental assent to overwhelming evidence; it is a God-given energy. In my youthful ministry, I was enamored with a set of books by Harry Rimruer that used scientific explanations to prove the veracity of God's Word. God was "proved" from nature, and at the time I felt such instruction was faith-producing. I had to live a few more years before I realized that faith based solely upon reason is not the character of Bible faith. No faith is needed if something has been proven.

In his book *An Expository Dictionary of New Testament Words*, W. E. Vine defines the New Testament word for faith, *pistis*, as "primarily a firm persuasion, a conviction based upon hearing (akin to *peitho*, to persuade): it is used in the New Testament always of faith in God or Christ, or things spiritual." Faith, as the Bible uses the word, rests upon the character of God and requires no proof other than the moral perfections of the One who cannot lie. Even if the statement contradicts our five senses and violates the sensible conclusions of logic, believers continue to believe—by faith. Convinced of this, Paul cried out, "Let God be true but every man a liar…" (Romans 3:4).

God approves of this response of faith, for it rises above proofs and rests in the very heart of God Himself.

In one of my earlier books, *Let Us See Jesus*, I wrote:

Faith is produced by God, not by man. Faith is a divine energy, not a religious one. It has its origin in the Godhead, not in the Body of Christ.

We're not capable of producing this dynamic of faith, only of receiving it. In the same manner that homeowners don't produce electricity, but only consume it, we do not produce faith; we only utilize it. Furthermore, the generator that produced electricity does not consume it, but only transmits it. Similarly, God does not produce faith to consume it, but to transmit it. We receive faith not to learn how to produce it, but to learn how to release it.

Faith's source is in God the Father, God the Son and God the Holy Spirit, not in the Bible, not in theology, not in doctrine, although sometimes doctrine is called "the faith." The Bible, theology, and doctrine will direct faith, but will not produce it.

Faith is not even produced by prayer, fasting, or words, though these might release faith. Fasting for faith might produce a weight loss, and working for faith may bring about exhaustion, but faith is not produced by man's efforts; its source is totally in God. "God has dealt to each one a measure of faith" (Romans 12:3*b*).

Faith does not have its origins in the heart of humanity, but in the word of God. Faith is a heavenly grace made available by God's mercy through His inspired Word. Paul was aware of this, for he wrote, "So then faith comes by hearing, and hearing by the word of God" (Romans 10:17), and the Greek word Paul used for "the word of God" is *rhema*, which emphasizes the speaking of the word rather than the thing that is spoken. It is while God is talking—while the speaking is going on—that faith is transmitted. Faith comes by way of the voice channel of God. Divine energy accompanies God's voice, and the Bible calls that energy "faith."

The spoken word of God is the source of true faith. This is declared plainly in the Bible. It was often illustrated by Christ as He spoke to the needy one who responded immediately; it was testified to by those great heroes of faith listed in the eleventh chapter of Hebrews who followed God "to the brink" after they had heard a word from God. God's living Word (Jesus Christ), God's written Word (the Bible) and God's preached word are all intended to produce, inspire, and direct faith. But it is not the historical account of God's Logos (Jesus Christ), the dead letter of the written Word, nor even the oratory of preachers that produces divine faith in us; it is the living word, which emanates from the presence of God Himself, that changes our atmosphere into His atmosphere, our doubts into His confidence, and our fears into His faith. It is God's word on the wings of His Spirit—through whatever channel He may choose—that illuminates our darkness, dispels our doubts, and infuses us with His faith. The Word without the Spirit becomes law, but the law with the Spirit produces faith.

Of course, persons are required to be participants in this change from an absence of faith to a fullness of faith. Paul declared that "hearing" is an essential condition to the reception of faith. No amount of divine speaking will be effectual until there is a genuine hearing. It is not how often or how forcefully the message has been proclaimed, but in what measure it has really been heard that determines the level of faith in any believer's life.

If faith is to be produced in our hearts, we must listen to the Word of God as intently as a person listens to a will being read or with as much interest as the accused waiting to hear

> While it is possible to come into the presence of God outside of the prayer channel, the very purpose of prayer is to "come before the throne of grace."

the sentence of the judge. What is being said will affect us for eternity; this is the eternal God speaking and imparting the atmosphere of His eternity into our limited sphere of *now*. Careless listening will produce human frailty not divine faith.

Since God is "...the author and finisher of our faith..." (Hebrews 12:2), we need to spend time in His presence to receive that faith. While it is possible to come into the presence of God outside of the prayer channel, the very purpose of prayer is to "come before the throne of grace." If, when we are in His presence, we rise above our self-centeredness and genuinely seek Him, faith will flow from God to us. This faith will, in turn, greatly energize our prayers and enhance our relationship with God.

When I was in the third grade, I wanted badly what was then called an Irish Mall. It was a cart propelled by the rider, who alternately pulled and pushed a handle connected to a rod that moved between his legs. This contraption was steered with one's feet. It was a child's version of a railroad cart. I asked for one for Christmas, but since we were in the midst of the Great Depression, it seemed impossible that my petition would be answered.

A few weeks before Christmas, my parents left me at home to babysit my brothers and sisters while they went to church. As the car pulled out of the driveway, my mother instructed me to go into the attic, get down the Christmas decorations, and begin trimming the tree in the front room. When I climbed up into the attic, I was surprised to see a bright, shiny Irish Mall in the corner. Dad had found a used one and had painted it beautifully. I never mentioned my discovery to my parents, but each evening during family prayer, I prayed with amazing faith for an Irish Mall for Christmas. My "faith" was greatly enhanced by knowing what my parents had provided for me.

When prayer brings us into the presence of God and our spirits get quiet enough to hear the voice of God speaking to us, we will discover what He

> Faith interacts with God, the one great reality who is the source of existence for all things.

intends to do and our "faith" is magnified beyond controllable proportions. We believe easily for what is unseen in our natural world. Why? Because we have seen it with our spiritual eyes. Faith sees into the unseeable, but it does not see the nonexistent. Faith interacts with God, the one great reality who is the source of existence for all things. God's promises—His Word—always conform to reality, and the person who trusts them enters a world of fact as God declares things to be—not a world of fantasy as we might wish to see things.

The false prophets declared the fantasy of Jerusalem's preservation, but Jeremiah, who was in communication with God, declared that the city would be destroyed and its inhabitants taken captive. He lamented over this message. He would have preferred that the other prophets be true and himself the liar; but, having been in the presence of God, he had touched actuality rather than illusion. Knowing the reality of impending captivity enabled Jeremiah to pray effectively and counsel the people truthfully. His message may have violated their desires, but it revealed the divine purposes. This kind of faith comes from hearing God during prayer times when we are seeking Him rather than things.

All the provisions of Christ's atonement flow to individuals through the energy of faith. The indwelling Holy Spirit and all forgiveness, cleansing, regeneration, and answers to prayer are received by faith. God has not provided an alternative way. This necessary faith is a gift of God, and it is a miracle. It is the ability God gives us to trust His Son.

Arthur W. Pink, in his book *An Exposition of Hebrews*, writes about this wonderful spiritual energy the Bible calls faith:

> Faith shuts its eyes to all that is seen, and opens its ears to all God has said. Faith is a convictive power which overcomes carnal reasonings, carnal prejudices, and carnal excuses. It enlightens the judgment, molds the heart, moves the will, and reforms the life. It takes us off earthy things and worldly vanities, and occupies us with spiritual and Divine realities. It emboldens against discouragements, laughs at difficulties, resists the Devil, and triumphs over temptations. It does so because it unites the soul to God and draws strength from Him.
>
> Thus faith is altogether a supernatural thing.

If, indeed, "faith is altogether a supernatural thing"—a gift of God—why is it that we see so little of its fruit in our congregations and in the lives of individual Christians?

It is never because the faith is impotent, for every gift of God is perfect. It must be because God's faith is so seldom released. It is not my gift of money to my grandchildren that buys the special treat; it is when they release that money to the clerk that it becomes a medium of exchange, allowing them to possess what their hearts desire. Similarly, God's imparted faith must be released in order to receive God's promised blessings. Prayer is the channel for both the reception and the release of faith.

Back in 1929, William James wrote the book *The Varieties of Religious Experience* in which he noted, "Through prayer, religion insists, things which cannot be realized in any other manner come about: energy which but for prayer would be bound is by prayer set free and operates in some part, be it objective or subjective, of the world of facts."

In the New Testament, this release of faith is called believing. Because the same Greek word forms the root for *faith* and *believe*, these two words are so integrally connected that it is difficult to think of them separately, but it is desirable to do so. Faith is a noun, while believe is a verb. A noun names a person, place, or thing, while a verb gives action to that person, place, or thing. The verb does not stand or substitute for the noun but gives motion to it. Hence, "believe" cannot always and probably very seldom should stand for "faith." The two work together, but they cannot substitute for one another. Faith, as a divine commitment, requires believing as a human confession of God's committal.

If faith is a force received, believing is our releasing of that force. Perhaps it would be fair to say that faith is God's attitude shared with humans, while believing is our action based on that attitude. Faith is an assurance, and

> Faith is trust; believing is obeying. Faith is a God-given ordinance; believing is our observing that ordinance.

believing is assenting to it. Faith is an affirmation; believing is an admitting. Faith is the confidence; believing is the credence. Faith is trust; believing is obeying. Faith is a God-given ordinance; believing is our observing that ordinance.

If faith is a reliance, then believing would be a responding. If faith is a persuasion, then believing must be performing.

Robert Girdlestone, in his book *Synonyms and Antonyms of the Old Testament*, states, "The man who believes God is he

93

who, having received a revelation from Him, realizes it, and acts upon it as true."

It would be doctrinally and practically accurate to say that faith is the eye of the soul, which looks out toward God's promises and represents them clearly and convincingly to us; believing is the action of the soul, which lays hold of the contents of those promises and applies them to human behavior.

Since faith has its source in God and is channeled through prayer, as He speaks to us, it is the developing of

> Intellectual assent and spiritual faith are not on the same level.

a more intimate relationship with God that increases one's faith—not the enlarging of one's intellectual understanding or emotional response.

Intellectual assent and spiritual faith are not on the same level. My religious background made little provision for the security of the believer. Somehow I had come to believe that Christ saved me from my sins, but it was completely up to me to keep myself saved. In my Bible college days, one of my instructors convinced me of the Bible's assurance that, "He which hath begun a good work in you will perform it until the day of Jesus Christ" (Philippians 1:6).

I searched many other Scriptures and gave assent to God's great provision of security in the faith, but it did not give me the inner assurance or peace I craved. One day in my prayer time, the Lord seemed to fold me in His arms and hold me close to His chest. Such love flowed from Him to me. As I wept in His presence, He whispered to me, "There is no way I would let you get away from Me."

Faith flowed into my being like water released from a dam. I no longer had to make myself believe. Divine faith had replaced intellectual faith. God had me securely in His grasp, and there was no power on earth or hell that could pluck me out of His hand. Peace replaced my fear, and joy replaced my anxiety. Theological faith had been replaced with God's faith that comes from hearing Him speak.

Quite frequently, we hear preachers proclaim, "What we

need is more faith," but one wonders if we actually need more faith or more believing. Truth, no matter how reinforced it may be, does not vitally affect our lives until we act on that truth with obedience, joyful praise, or active participation in the promise. Belief gives action to our faith, and this is most likely to happen during times of prayer.

Remember that Jesus said, "...Whatever things you ask when you pray, believe that you receive them, and you will have them" (Mark 11:24). The

> One wonders if we actually need more faith or more believing.

time to believe is during prayer. Attempting to pray now and believe later is ineffectual. It is always far easier to believe when we are in the Divine Presence than when we are in the midst of affliction.

Faith, the divine energy received, and believing, the releasing of that energy, are inseparable. They are coupled together like marriage and loving or clouds and raining. It is the first (faith) that induces the second (believing), and when they are properly blended, they produce a third quotient; something happens.

Faith is received by hearing God speak, and our believing is released by speaking that word back to God or to the problem. Jesus said, "...Whoever says to this mountain, 'Be removed and cast into the sea,' and does not doubt in his heart, but believes that those things he says will be done, he will have whatever he says. Therefore I say to you, whatever things you ask when you pray, believe that you receive them, and you will have them" (Mark 11:23,24).

When I was pastoring in Eugene, Oregon, we outgrew our facility and needed desperately to enlarge. To meet zoning requirements, however, it was necessary for us to purchase the property next door to use for additional parking. The owners refused to sell, for they had purchased that house as investment property, and they intended to live off the rental in their old age.

When I shared this impasse with the congregation in mid-week prayer service, they joined me in importunate prayer.

God told us, "Don't cry out to Me. I have given that property. Possess it in faith."

The next day, I made an appointment with the owners of the land and drove some fifty miles to talk with the husband and wife. I informed them that God had declared that He had given us that property. Since they were not professing Christians, I told them that I was confident that God would indemnify them for the loss of title to the land, and I asked them to set a price on their property. Just a week previously, they said, they had rejected an offer for the land, and they told me the amount of money they had turned down. Once again, they assured me that there was no way I could induce them to sell that corner lot to the church.

On the drive back to my study, I praised the Lord continually for what He was going to do. I had conflicting facts before me, for God said that He had given us the land, but the owners refused to release it to us. However, I hadn't been in my study more than an hour when I received a phone call from the owners saying that they were in agreement to sell me the land, and they stated a price that was many thousands of dollars below the offer they had refused a week earlier. When I asked why they had changed their minds, they hesitantly said that God had come into their house and spoken to both of their hearts; they were afraid of disobeying God's voice.

The faith for this purchase was God's not mine. But the faith which was released in going to the problem and speaking that word of faith perpetrated a dramatic change in circumstances that made it possible for us to have the full title of that property before the week was ended. Holding that promise before the Lord in my praise kept it fervent, alive, and active until the intended result was manifested. All of this was the result of prayer.

Prayer Resists Doubt

When Paul exhorted young Timothy, he challenged him to "fight the good fight of faith" (1 Timothy 6:12a). Even though faith is a divine energy that comes as a gift from God and is released in our believing, it has an enemy. Whether that enemy surfaces from within our lives or opposes us from without, the name of that enemy is doubt. In the Garden of Eden, the serpent's approach to Eve was to instill a doubt by asking, "Has God indeed said...?" (Genesis 3:1). His tactics are unchanged today. He need not refute what God has said if he can successfully implant a doubt in our minds. As we well know, faith and doubt cannot get along. They don't belong together. There is a constant warfare between them, and one will always subdue the other. Faith embraces both the veracity of God's nature and His Word, but doubt questions the faithfulness and integrity of God.

Doubt is an inherent danger in every act of faith. Seasoned Christians know that whenever they declare that they are trusting God to perform His promises they will soon hear a voice whispering, "But what if He doesn't...?" One of the fatal characteristics of doubt is that it presumes that what we see, hear, feel, and taste in this world is real, and what God speaks of in His spiritual kingdom is unreal. But if God says something is real, not only is it real, but by faith we can reach into His realm and make it become a living reality in our world of sense and space. To do this, however, we must conquer doubt.

> One of the fatal characteristics of doubt is that it presumes that what we see, hear, feel, and taste in this world is real, and what God speaks of in His spiritual kingdom is unreal.

Doubt, as the word is used in the New Testament, is a wavering, a hesitance, or a staggering in faith. It is not unbelief; it is more a poor handling of belief. It is somewhat like trying to tune in a weak radio station; it wavers in and out, often growing less and less discernible. It is not by accident that Jesus called Peter "of little faith" before asking him why he doubted while walking on the water. The "stronger station" of the boisterous waves overpowered the signal of faith that was transmitted when Jesus said, "Come" (see Matthew 14:22-33).

Doubt is uncertainty about God's promises; doubt lacks confidence in the God of those promises and considers their fulfillment very unlikely. Doubt puts our experience over against God's Word and trusts our reasoning more than the reality of God's Word. Doubting is not the drawing back of apostasy; it is simply hesitating,

> Doubt is not honest inquiry; it is a wavering in faith after faith has come.

reexamining, or questioning what has already been proven. It is not honest inquiry; it is a wavering in faith after faith has come. As such, doubt is the most deadly enemy of faith, for it dissipates faith after faith has been received. Peter didn't doubt until he had walked on the water for quite a distance. The other disciples, to whom the word of faith was not addressed, were not condemned for doubting; they were totally without faith for water-walking.

Doubt is always costly, but it is especially costly when it becomes a dominant force in the moment of crisis. Ironically, this same doubt can prevent our participating in victory even after the battle has been won.

When God speaks, faith flows and we generally believe and obey. But in the action of obedience, our minds often rationalize the situation, producing doubts that can totally short-circuit our faith and make it of no effect. The old cliché is well worth remembering: *Never doubt in the darkness what you trusted in the light.* The time for double-checking is when God is speaking. Once we get into the battle, it is too late to try to determine if God has indeed said. (See Genesis 3:1.) Having put our hands to the plow, it is too late to look back. If obedience was an act of faith, then doubt will stop faith's action. It will soon produce disobedience, and great will be the penalty thereof.

Is anyone of us immune to doubts? Once the sweet song of God's voice is replaced with the croaking of the frogs in the blackness of the night, doesn't every heart skip a beat in hesitancy? The key to dispelling doubt seems to be this: Review consistently what produced the faith within us in the first place. Revive the relationship through prayer, review the promises made, renew the commitment given, and doubt can gain no foothold.

The fight of faith is waged in prayer. The way to overcome the word of doubt is with the "word of faith" which "is near you, even in your mouth and in your heart" (Romans 10:8). If faith came through praying, it can be preserved through continued prayer. Since faith flows when God speaks, we will do well to remain in His presence to hear His voice during the dark seasons when doubt demands an audience.

> Since faith flows when God speaks, we will do well to remain in His presence to hear His voice during the dark seasons when doubt demands an audience.

If faith and doubt are mortal enemies, we need to have a constant increasing and strengthening of our faith, lest the doubts induced by our natural life overcome our faith in God. The more time we spend in God's presence, the stronger our confidence and trust in Him will become.

Faith, not fear, is God's gift to us; trust, not doubt, is God's expectation from us. As we spend time in God's presence, the eternal battle between faith and doubt is settled in favor of faith, for how can we doubt God when we are in His presence? When faith has conquered doubt, our prayer moves from the skirmishes of conflict to submission of conduct. We cease contesting our concepts and enter into the conquest of our wills.

For Reflection
1. If faith's source is in God, what channel does He use to impart it to us?
2. If faith is effective only when released, where can faith best be released?
3. Do you ever have any doubts about God and His Word? How do you resolve them?

rayer Ascends As the Channel for Submission

Since Paul declared that our salvation is a matter of declaring the lordship of Jesus with our mouths and believing in His resurrection with our hearts (see Romans 10:9,10), submission to that lordship becomes the prerequisite for living victorious Christian lives. God's gift of faith gives us a calm confidence in His character, and this enables us to submit the conduct of our lives to His plan and purpose. This submission is easier to preach than practice, for our self-centered natures struggle to have their own way.

No person on the face of this earth has ever lived a life as surrendered to the will of God as Jesus Christ. He testified that He always did the will of the Father, that He spoke only the words He heard His Father speak, and that He did only the deeds He saw His Father do. He came in the will of the Father to do the will of the Father, and nothing that humanity or demons could throw at Him deterred Him for one moment. However, just prior to His arrest and crucifixion, He went to the Garden of Gethsemane to pray. "He began to be sorrowful and deeply distressed...and fell on His face, and prayed, saying, 'O My Father, if it is possible, let this cup pass from Me; nevertheless, not as I will, but as You will'" (Matthew 26:37*b*,39). This time, submission to the will of God was difficult and distressful.

The Bible does not record the nature of the inner conflict of Christ. It tells us only that it was with great agony of soul that Jesus could submit. Why was this so difficult? Certainly, it was not facing merely the pain of crucifixion, for thousands of martyrs faced such a death with songs and testimonies of victory. No, it wasn't the pain, ignominy, or even the shame of the cross that so troubled Jesus. It was having to become our sin-bearer. "He [God] made Him who knew no sin to be sin for us, that we might become the righteousness of God in Him" (2 Corinthians 5:21). As our substitute, Jesus, although absolutely sinless Himself, had to taste and conquer sin and then pay the penalty it deserved—death.

Even to begin to understand Christ's agony, we need to review the nature of sin. Most of what we

> Rebellion began in heaven, not on the earth.

catalog as sin is merely a manifestation of sin. True sin is rebellion against the known will of God. It began in heaven, not on the earth. The highest of God's creation—the angel who was in charge of protecting the holiness of God as the anointed cherub—expressed his will against the will of God.

Isaiah 14 tells us that Lucifer, known to us as the devil or Satan, exerted his will against God five separate times. This was the first exercise of any will other than the will of the Father, and it caused great confusion in the kingdom of God. When Lucifer declared that he would be above God—actually replacing God—he was expelled from heaven, and God created a brief parenthetical break in eternity. We call it *time*. This is the season where God contains all wills that oppose His will. When all wills finally surrender to the will of God, "time shall be no more."

In spite of our delight in declaring, "The devil made me do it," the Bible teaches that the root of sin is the exercise of self-will against the will of God. In looking with prophetic insight at the work of Christ on Calvary, Isaiah wrote, "All we like sheep have gone astray; we have turned, every one, to *his own way*, and the Lord has laid on Him the iniquity of us all" (Isaiah 53:6, italics added). Once this root of sin begins to grow, the fruit of sin begins to mature. Christ, agonizing over tasting rebellion against the Father, knew that if this was not conquered, we would never be acceptable to God or comfortable in heaven. God hates rebellion so deeply that He declared through His prophet Samuel, "For rebellion is as the sin of witchcraft, and stubbornness is as iniquity and idolatry" (1 Samuel 15:23*a*).

God still views the exertion of any will against His own will as the work of the devil— whether it is done directly by Satan or indirectly by

> Insisting upon our own way is participating in the works of the devil.

us. We need not be a member of a coven of witches to be involved in witchcraft. In God's view, insisting upon our own way is participating in the works of the devil. Since this is true, submission to the will of God becomes the first rule of Christian behavior. It will not always be easy, but it will always be right.

Jesus conquered His revulsion against tasting rebellion and surrendered His will to the Father in the prayer channel. He did not subdue His will through counseling, talking with friends, or by deep inner meditation. He prayed to the Father and, being assured that this was the center of the divine will, He submitted. From this moment on, there was no wavering of commitment. His surrender was absolute and final.

There comes a time in our prayer lives when we cease dealing with our will, wants, and wishes and face the will of God. When He impresses that will upon our hearts, we remain in His presence, allowing Him to communicate with us by His indwelling Spirit. We soften. Our wills crumble, and we, like Jesus, find ourselves saying, "Not my will, but Thine be done." This rarely happens to the nonpraying person, for it is during times of communion with God that His two greatest softening agents are allowed to work: faith and love.

Faith at Work During Prayer

Faith is far more than an attitude; it is an energy at work. James said, "I will show you my faith by my works," and, speaking of Abraham, said, "Do you see that faith was working together with his works, and by works faith was made perfect?" (James 2:18,22). Faith is not manifested by mere words, but by methodical action. In the great faith chapter of the Bible (Hebrews 11), the statement "By faith..." is always followed by a description of action. For instance, we read, "By faith Abraham obeyed when he was called to go out to the place which he would afterward receive as an inheritance" (Hebrews 11:8*a*). His submission and obedience were expressions of his faith in God.

I grew up with this principle displayed before me. My parents walked away from an established business to become pastors of small lumber town churches in the Northwest. This was during the Great Depression when the only available work was with the government-sponsored WPA, and clergy weren't accepted into that program. Although they never doubted their call into the ministry, they had to believe just to put a meal on the table for the five children. Over and over again, I would hear my mother's voice singing, "Trust and obey, for there's no other way, to be happy in Jesus, but to trust and obey." My parents never expected to understand God's reasons, but they did implicitly obey His requests. They did not believe it possible to separate trust from obedience. Neither does God.

The word *obey* is used by the translators of the Old Testament to express more fully the verb "to hear." It signifies the right response to the voice or the word of God. To hear is to be persuaded and to be persuaded is to obey. To the prophets and priests who heard from God, receiving divine utterances in a noncommittal or passive fashion was out of the question. Obedience was expected of them and by them. One either obeyed or resisted God's voice actively, which is called "rebellion" in the Old Testament and "disobedience" in the New Testament. The patriarchs, prophets, and poets of the Old Testament showed and stated that the proper and fitting response to God's initiative is humble acquiescence, active obedience, and unconditional submission and trust.

The brokenhearted cry of God throughout the entire Old Testament was because of the disobedience of His people. No matter how He blessed them, communicated with them, and provided for them, they took what they wanted and still did as they pleased. They were selfish and self-centered, stubborn and sinful. At times, it seems that they would rather have climbed a tree in disobedience than stood on the ground in obedience.

All who have walked with God and have entered into a

prayer partnership with Him will agree: Not all of His commands are pleasant and agreeable. The command for Noah to build an ark carried with it the horrible awareness of the destruction of life. Abraham must have felt an inner revulsion at God's command to sacrifice Isaac, and Moses had many years of unpleasantness because of God's call to lead the Israelites out of Egypt. But pleasant or not, they obeyed.

God speaks not only of health, wealth, and happiness, but also of suffering, privation, and labor. We must respond to every

> We cannot pick and choose what we want to obey.

word of God with either a positive or a negative reaction. We either will or will not obey. There is no neutral position, nor is there ever an acceptable substitute for complete obedience, as King Saul learned when he obeyed the Lord only partially and sought to make up for it by offering a massive sacrifice to God. "To obey is better than sacrifice, and to heed than the fat of rams," God told him through the prophet (1 Samuel 15:22b). Because of this attempt to substitute sacrifice for obedience, God took the kingdom away from Saul and his progeny. We cannot pick and choose what we want to obey.

Obedience may be difficult at times, but disobedience is deadly at all times! The purpose of the gift of faith is to enable us to conform in humility to that which God prescribes either by claim or by promise. No other response is acceptable to God. Great faith demands complete submission and obedient behavior. The person who claims to possess great faith but does not live surrendered to God's will and word is deceived and quickly becomes a deceiver of others.

Faith not only demands surrender to the will of God; it undergirds and energizes that acquiescence. In a series of communications from God, first in my own heart and then confirmed through words given to me in three separate countries of the world, I moved from Atlanta to Phoenix, Arizona. God had told me the city to move to, the month that a house would be made available to me, and the month in which I would actually move. It entailed moving away from the two daughters who, until three years earlier, had spent their entire married lives in Argentina. We were enjoying them as neighbors and we were getting acquainted with the eight grandchildren we had seen far too seldom. The move was not a pleasant prospect for either my wife or me, but God made it clear that this was His will for us. Everything that God said to us came to pass in the very months that He had designated. We purchased the house He seemed to indicate, and we moved at the very end of the year.

Because we were obeying the Lord in this action, rather than functioning in our own desire levels, we were convinced that He would take care of all details. We put our Georgia house in the hands of a Christian realtor, assured that it would sell very rapidly; and we signed a contract agreeing to pay for the Phoenix house in six months.

I have never before seen such seller's remorse as I saw in the man who sold us the Phoenix house. He wanted it back and even tendered us an offer to repurchase it that would have given us a comfortable profit. But because we were convinced that God had directed us to this specific house, we refused to sell it back to him. His real estate agent told us that we had better have our payment in full on the due date—or they would happily repossess the house.

Months went by and I couldn't even give away my house in Georgia. Offers were made, but when I accepted them, the offers were withdrawn. As we got closer and closer to the deadline, I began to feel desperate.

> The Spirit would remind me of the faithfulness of God and ask me if God would begin a process that He was unable to complete.

I approached the banks, but since I was new to the area and had no "provable" source of income (bankers do not understand "living by faith"), I could not secure financing. My wife and I fought panic. We stood to lose the sizable down payment we had put on the house plus all the money we had spent upgrading it. Our prayers got desperate, but God did not answer us.

Every time I went to prayer over the situation, I was undergirded with the awareness of God's nature. The Spirit would remind me of the faithfulness of God and ask me if God would begin a process that He was unable to complete. Slowly, my confidence in God ascended high enough that, although I did not have an assurance that this financial need would be met on schedule, I could rest upon the very nature of a faithful God whose word I had obeyed in moving.

About six weeks before the deadline, I flew into Fort Worth, Texas, to speak at a convention. I was taken to my motel room and told that I would be picked up for the first service in about two hours. Feeling the desperateness of my circumstance, I threw myself across the bed and heard myself say, "God, this is the last time I am going to remind You of my predicament. If You want the house in Georgia to remain vacant and be destroyed by vandals, so be it. I purchased it with your money, so it will be Your loss. Furthermore, if You do not provide the funds to clear the note on my house in Phoenix, amen! You can only reduce me to nothing, and that is exactly what I had when I entered the ministry. My wife and I can start over. From now on, I am simply going to praise Your name and enjoy Your nature. You do whatever You want to do." It was a spiritual breakthrough for me. My joy returned, and I thoroughly enjoyed that conference as God met with us in a very special way.

Less than a month before the deadline, I received a phone call from my selling agent in Atlanta saying that he had an offer on my house. It needed an immediate response. All transactions were done by telephone and telegraph, and two weeks after his initial phone call, I had full cash from the sale of my house in Georgia. I was then able to pay off the note on my Phoenix house—one week early.

This whole experience had been a testing time during which God seemed to remain silent, yet the faith that His Spirit inspired quieted my fears and strengthened my heart to know that God would act according to His character. I had said *yes* to the will of God, and He undergirded that decision with His faith until all the details could be completed. This faith did not flow when I was talking to bankers; it functioned while I was talking to God in prayer. When faith is at work during times of prayer, we are able to maintain consecrations and submissions made to God even when existing circumstances do not seem to substantiate the will of God.

Love at Work During Prayer

Whether we like to admit it or not, we are inherently selfish creatures set on having our own way. When we are confronted with the will of God, which is often diametrically opposed to our personal wills, stubbornness rises in our hearts instead of submission to God's desires. Religion's consistent answer to this self-assertiveness has always been enforced law, but God prefers to envelop us in His love. While law may force us to comply, love entices us to yield. God does not compel us to conform to patterns; He loves us until we are transformed by His person. Pressure may cause us to do, but love can cause us to desire to do, and this is God's highest goal for our behavior. David wrote, "I delight to do Your will, O my God, and Your law is within my heart" (Psalm 40:8), and this is quoted and applied to Jesus in Hebrews 10:7. Christ came to fulfill the law, but He held that law in His heart. His responses were love responses; "I delight to do Your will" was His testimony.

In speaking of Christ's self-emptying and complete submission to the will of God, even though it meant death by crucifix-

> While law may force us to comply, love entices us to yield.

ion, Paul admonishes us, "Let this mind be in you which was also in Christ Jesus" (Philippians 2:5). God has sufficient pressure available to force us all to do what He wants us to do, but He does not present Himself as an autocratic despot who must be obeyed or severe penalties will be enforced. Rather He presents Himself as a Father who wants His children to respond to His will out of a love motivation. Accordingly, He works from within us, rather than by applying pressure outside of us. Paul declares, "It is God who works in you both to will and to do for His good pleasure" (Philippians 2:13). God loves us into submission, implants in us a strong desire to do what He desires, and then releases us to do "His good pleasure."

108

A man who would ask a young lady to clean his house, cook his meals, wash his clothes, and incubate his babies would be ridiculed and rebuffed. But, if that same man expressed his love rather than his needs, a woman might well marry him and willingly take over such responsibilities as an expression of her love for him. The burden of the request would be greatly lightened by the flow of love.

There is probably no time when a Christian's awareness of God's love is greater than when in His presence during seasons of prayer. That prayer time may well begin with a confession of sin and the expression of petitions for divine intervention. However, as our praying moves into the realm of communication with God by the help of the Holy Spirit, divine faith is released in our hearts, and a flow of love is primed. The more we express our love to God, the greater we yearn to do what is pleasing to Him.

Prayer may well begin with, "This is what I would have You do, O God." But if we remain in the secret place with Him long enough, we will alter that prayer to say, "What would You have me do, O Lord?" Love ceases to seek our desires and submits to His desires automatically and completely.

The church at Corinth was reminded, "Christ's love compels us" (2 Corinthians 5:14, NIV). Saunders translates this: "The love of Christ overwhelms us. It over-

> Because of His divine lovingkindness, we cease to contend for our wills and become content with God's will.

masters us, buoys us up, and carries us on." We must flee or fall before this love. As our wills crumble before this onslaught of divine lovingkindness, we are transformed; we were once slaves to self but we become submissive sons and daughters. We cease to contend for our wills and become content with God's will. We no longer demand our rights but desire His righteousness. Our response to love becomes a flow of life, even to the point that the things we once loved, we learn to hate; the things we once hated, we learn to love. This change from self-centeredness to Christ-centeredness is always transforming, for the object of our love becomes the controller of our lives.

If you've reared children, you may have been amazed to watch a self-centered, selfish child, who could hardly be forced to clean his or her bedroom, fall in love and suddenly become deeply concerned with another person's will. The interest of that object of love becomes the main interest for this formerly ego-centered person. Similarly, we may come brazenly into God's presence to plead our rights; but, after a short time of fellowship with Him who is all love and tenderness, we lose our arrogance and pride and bow down humbly to cry, "My Lord and my God." Accordingly, the Ephesian Christians were challenged to "walk in love, as Christ also has loved us and given Himself for us, an offering and a sacrifice to God for a sweet-smelling aroma" (Ephesians 5:2).

Love has always been life's greatest motivation to submit one to another. It helps put us in a right relationship with both ourselves and with others. None who spend time regularly with God in prayer can maintain a proud self-assertive attitude, for God's love melts us into submission; and when we see ourselves in contrast to Him, we join Paul in declaring, "I know that in me (that is, in my flesh) nothing good dwells" (Romans 7:18a). Spiritual pride is especially odious because it evidences a separation from the presence of God. The person who will pray long enough to reach the level of submission will walk in true humility. Such a person will have a correct self-image and awareness that all he has become is because of the love of God that dwells deep in his heart.

When we Christians learn to pray consistently the prayer of submission, we also learn to live the "amen" life. Whatever God suggests is met with

Love blossoms and bears fruit through association, not separation.

an immediate "OK," which is what "amen" means. We discover that the closer we walk with God, the more we know His mind and will for our lives, and experience has taught us that His way is always best for us. Sometimes, however, that will so opposes our wants that we say "good-bye" rather than "amen." We separate ourselves from His presence so we can

110

have our own way—without guilt. We may continue to manifest spiritual giftings, but we cease to flow in God's love.

"Absence makes the heart grow fonder" is far from the truth. Someone who had obviously lived a few years added, "...of someone else." Love blossoms and bears fruit through association, not separation. The more frequent and intimate the relationship, the more likely it is to mature and last. It is one thing to come into a love relationship with God, and it is quite another thing to maintain the fervency, devotion, and commitment of that love over a protracted season of time.

When I was a preacher, I was occasionally approached by a parishioner who confided that he didn't feel the love for his wife that he once had. My standard approach to this was to encourage him to take his wife on a short trip to have some quality time with her. This usually solved the problem. In being together without the interruptions of business or children, the former flow of love returned. They had not ceased loving each other; they had merely ceased taking the time to express their love to each other. Like the husband who works such long hours to support his wife and family that he has no time to share their lives, many Christian workers exhaust themselves in activity without budgeting time to enjoy a relationship with Christ Jesus. In Christ's letter to the church of Ephesus, He said, "Nevertheless, I have this against you, that you have left your first love" (Revelation 2:4). They had not "lost" their love for God; they had abandoned it in their pursuit of earthly responsibilities. Perhaps they had become so busy working for God that they didn't have time to be with God.

The prayer channel should be guarded as a lifeline to this love relationship with God. On Mars Hill, Paul told the Athenians, "In Him [Christ Jesus] we live and move and have our being" (Acts 17:28a), and it is prayer that keeps us in this vital and viable relationship with God. Time spent in reading the Word and in praying should be more than religious discipline. It should be an investment in our relationship with God in which we walk and talk with God in seasons of receiving and returning His love.

Submission at Work During Prayer

Since there is nothing in our "flesh" that enjoys praying, the very act of praying is submission to God. During my many years of prayer, I have discovered that, no matter what posture I assume while praying, my muscles cramp and complain. My mind wanders. I get sleepy and feel hungry. I can count on needing a restroom. Prayer is warfare. I am confident that I am not alone in this conflict. The initial battling is not with Satan; it is with our human, natural self-life. The redeemed spirit within us wants to submit to God, but every other part of us screams for attention.

The issue is this: To whom will we submit? Will we discipline ourselves to answer God's call to prayer, or will we succumb to the insistent demands of our bodies? Most prayerlessness is because the physical wins over the spiritual. We submit to the wrong stimuli. If He is allowed, the Holy Spirit will help us win this struggle, but this requires submitting to His will rather than trying to win the victory by use of our own willpower.

The pristine example of submission is, of course, our Lord Jesus in Gethsemane. Mark records His words as, "Abba, Father, all things are possible for You. Take this cup away from Me; nevertheless, not what I will, but what You will" (Mark 14:36). It is significant that Jesus prayed this prayer of submission three times. (See Matthew 26:44.) After each session of prayer, He was at peace with Himself and with God. But when He went to share the first two victories with the disciples whom He had asked to pray with Him and found them sound asleep, He had to return to His place of prayer and fight the battle all over again.

If submission to the known will of God were a one-time act, far more persons would do it. Submission does require an initial "yes, Lord!" But it also requires a progressive surrender in the consistent outworking of God's will in our daily behavior.

> Unless what we say in the prayer of submission is backed up by consistent acts of compliance, we have not truly surrendered to God.

112

During prayer times of fellowship with God, we are motivated by faith and love to surrender to God's will. But often, when we later fellowship with other believers who are self-centered and severed from the will of God yet seem to be prosperous and happy, something within us cries, "It isn't fair." We withdraw our consecration because God requires so much of us.

Like Jesus after He rebuked His sleeping disciples, we, too, have to return to fellowship with the Father and resubmit to the will of God. Unless what we say in the prayer of submission is backed up by consistent acts of compliance, we have not truly surrendered to God. When our behavior revokes our surrender, we need to return to the place of prayer and once again hand our wills to the will of God. Jesus did, and we can too.

Is it possible that each time Jesus returned to find His disciples sleeping, He realized more fully what was entailed in taking on our sinful nature? It seems consistent for God not to ask us to consecrate ourselves to more than we can currently comprehend. As God enlarges our comprehension of what is involved, He requires more than a reconsecration; *He demands an additional consecration.*

I have often said publicly that if I had fully understood all that was involved in God's urgings to leave the pastorate to become an itinerant

> I had to return to my prayer closet and enlarge my surrender.

minister, I would still be pastoring. I know that I did not possess sufficient courage to consecrate myself to what I am now involved in. Mercifully, God merely unfolded one step at a time and asked me to take that step. First, He asked that I leave the security of a salary and a congregation that loved me to travel from church to church sharing the truths God had taught me about praise. This was traumatic, but God inspired faith and enveloped me with such love that I could not resist making a full surrender to His will.

When I learned some of the deceitful ways of a few persons in ministerial leadership, when some withheld offerings that had been designated for me, I faced a new revelation of some obstacles I would confront. I had to return to my prayer closet and enlarge my surrender.

As God shifted the emphasis of my message from praise to worship, I felt greater resistance to my message, receiving fewer and fewer repeat invitations. I was tempted to return to the message that had been so well-received, but when in the presence of the Lord in prayer, I submitted my will to preach what God was giving to me.

When God required me to sell my house and eventually move to the East Coast where I was totally unknown, I felt He was asking too much from me. Again, as I sought His face in prayer, my heart softened to His perfect will.

I resisted requests to write a book until, during prayer, the Lord let me know that this was His voice speaking to me through publishers. With my heavy traveling schedule, writing seemed out of the question. Besides, I was convinced that I had no talents in this area. I withheld my surrender to this task for a long time, but when I realized that it was hindering my fellowship with God, I gave in.

During the past calendar year, God spoke to me through His chosen channels in several different nations. Each time He has said that my greatest ministry is ahead of me—

> God doesn't reveal the next thing He wants us to do until we have done the *last* thing He told us to do.

not behind me. Several times He has said that everything up until now is but preparation for what He intends to do through me. I was hoping that I could taper off and get old, but now God is demanding a surrender of my will. I know that at whatever point I cease reaching into His presence during prayer, I will stagnate and further revelation will be stifled. None of us has yet arrived at God's perfect will for his or her life, so none of us has made the ultimate surrender to Him. God is content with the surrender of today, if He is assured that we will return to His presence tomorrow. As long as we seek His face, it is likely that we will continue to surrender to His will.

I have learned another principle about surrendering to God. God doesn't reveal the next thing He wants us to do until we have done the last thing He told us to do. We are not allowed to pick and choose what we will surrender to and what we will retain self-control over. Since God's revelation is progressive, it demands that our submission be consecutive. Jesus told the Jews in the temple at Jerusalem, "If anyone wills to do His will, he shall know concerning the doctrine" (John 7:17 *a*). God's promise of revelation is tied to our promise of submission. God will speak, if we will obey. God will lead, if we will follow. God will unfold His will, if we will embrace that will. The attitude of submission opens the door for God's intervention.

Since submission involves the heart as well as the head, it is most likely that we will submit during times of prayer—when our whole being is reaching out to God. At times my entire prayer time is spent grappling with submission. Sometimes I'm simply too tired or too lonely to go out on one more trip. Sometimes I must surrender areas of my thought life to God to enable Him to impart further spiritual truth to and through me. These times of prayer are not always battles of the will. Sometimes they reflect my inability to understand what God is seeking in me. Then as I continue to pour out my heart before Him, He is able to impress His will upon my heart. As that happens, my joyful response is, "Thy will be done."

Admittedly, however, my prayer time is occasionally a true conflict of wills. I must then extend my prayer until my spirit can genuinely say "amen!" to God's perfect will. Once the conflict is over and the surrender is complete, thanksgiving and praise well up in my soul, for true submission channels joy. When we submit, God assumes all responsibility for guidance, and He also assumes all consequences of that guidance. What a relief to our tired beings.

Submission also gives us courage and confidence. Knowing that God is now in charge of the issue, we have new courage to face life. We have surrendered our wills to the One who said, "'For My thoughts are not your thoughts, nor are your ways My ways,' says the Lord. 'For as the heavens are higher than the earth, so are My ways higher than your ways, and My

115

thoughts than your thoughts'" (Isaiah 55:8,9). This is not a statement of the will of God as much as it is an admission of the will of mankind. God yearns to bring us into His ways and to reveal His thoughts to us. The hindering factor is our self-will. When we surrender to the will and ways of the heavenly Father, we enter into His superior ways and knowledge as a matter of course.

Submission to the mind and heart of God also gives us confidence. Our surrender is to a Person, and God has never failed and will never fail us. Before submitting, we were never certain that our way was correct, but now we have absolute confidence in the ways of our Lord. This enables us to live positively even in the midst of extremely negative circumstances. We have heard from God. Knowing that He never makes a statement one day only to contradict it the next day, we depend confidently upon what He says. This is why submission to God brings us into a firm commitment to His Word. He cannot fail, and we dare not fail. His Word is a constant, so our surrender must be constant. When He enters into a covenant with us, all the resources of heaven back it up; so our covenant with Him needs the commitment of everything that is with us.

When prayers of petition give way to prayers of submission, they ascend gloriously; and our hearts can cry with Paul, "But thanks be to God, who gives us the victory through our Lord Jesus Christ" (1 Corinthians 15:57).

For Reflection

1. Does God's call to complete submission to His will go against the grain of your life?
2. How can prayer help us at times like this?
3. Does awareness of God's love make submission any easier for you?
4. Do you see submission to God as a positive or negative?

rayer Ascends As the Channel for Thanksgiving

The joy and peace that accompany moving into the perfect will of God lead us naturally into thanksgiving. Only the most ungrateful person would walk proudly in this new spiritual realm. We cannot help knowing that everything we enjoy in God has come as a gift from His hand, so we have no honest basis for pride. We do, however, have a genuine reason for thanksgiving. While giving thanks to God should be the automatic response of a redeemed life, true thankfulness is far rarer than one may suppose.

When I was a child, I was taught that the "magic" words that unlocked closed doors of personal relationships were *please* and *thank you.* I have found them as valuable in my relationship with God as in my relationship with people. *Thank you* is an admission that a gratuitous gift has been received. It calls for humility and acknowledges that another has met a need. It is the very least that can be done to repay another. Unfortunately, we Christians tend to take for granted many things that are done for us. We act as though we deserved them.

When I was a pastor, I used to schedule at least two communion services a year in which the bread was served as a large loaf from which communicants tore off a generous section. I then asked them to go through the church, offering to share their bread with another while expressing thanks for the contribution that person had made to their spiritual lives. I urged them to remember the church babysitters, the pianist and organist, the parking attendants, the ushers, the secretaries, the choir members and soloists and anyone else who, because of his or her consecration and service, had made worship easier. This service often ended in a tear-filled season of worship, as workers realized that they were appreciated and others realized the benefits they had received.

It's easy just to accept service without an expression of thanks, and this is true of our relationship with Jesus Christ. We become so accustomed to His gifts and graces that we feel that we deserve them. During the days that Jesus was on this earth...

> He entered a certain village, [and] there met Him ten men who were lepers, who stood afar off. And they lifted up their voices and said, "Jesus, Master, have mercy on us!" So when He saw them, He said to them, "Go, show yourselves to the priests." And so it was that as they went, they were cleansed. And one of them, when he saw that he was healed, returned, and with a loud voice glorified God, and fell down on his face at His feet, giving Him thanks. And he was a Samaritan. So Jesus answered and said, "Were there not ten cleansed? But where are the nine? Were there not any found who returned to give glory to God except this foreigner?" (Luke 17:12-18).

It may well be argued that the nine, being Jewish, were obeying Christ's command to show themselves to the priest for their ritualistic cleansing, but did this require such haste that they could not turn around and say, "Thank You"? Obeying a recent order does not negate a prior command. God had long ago mandated, "...Be thankful to Him, and bless His name. For the Lord is good; His mercy is everlasting..." (Psalm 100:4,5).

> Once we have our needs met by God, we tend to ignore Him until another need presses us.

These nine lepers had never risen above the level of petition in their prayer. They knew what they wanted, and they got into Christ's presence before making their petition. But once they obtained a favorable answer, they did not deal any further with Jesus. The lesson is recorded in the Bible, for it is a revelation of the selfishness in the human heart. Once we have our needs met by God, we tend to ignore Him until another need presses us.

In the introduction to his Roman letter, Paul establishes that God has revealed Himself to all generations of people, but the apostle says that the wrath of God has been revealed "because, although they knew God, they did not glorify Him as God, nor were thankful" (Romans 1:21*a*). Ingratitude separates us from God. Unthankful hearts open our lives to God's judgment rather than to His blessings. This is not because God's feelings are easily hurt. An unthankful heart evidences wrong thinking to us. If we have no thoughts of thanksgiving, our concerns are very self-centered and self-centeredness makes us feel that we deserve any good we receive. Wisely, Paul challenged the Christians in Colosse to "continue earnestly in prayer, being vigilant in it with thanksgiving" (Colossians 4:2).

Thanksgiving Is a Route Into God's Presence

It is wrong for us to view thanksgiving merely as a response to God. It is also a means of approach to God. We are invited to "enter into His gates with thanksgiving, and into His courts with praise. Be thankful to Him, and bless His name" (Psalm 100:4). The thankful heart has access to God when the needy heart is still trying to find Him. When need impels us to search for God, we are usually so overwhelmed with the pressing necessity that we wouldn't recognize God if He were standing beside us. The burdened and troubled seeker after God has tunnel vision. As such people push forward in their quest after God, they overlook all the beauties of His blessing, both past and present.

While need is often a route into God's presence, Scripture promises that thanksgiving will always be a route to God. I was once ministering in a congregation that seemed bound in spirit. The limited praise was anemic, and God's presence seemed far away. I stopped teaching and suggested that we pick a bouquet of thanksgiving to present to the Lord. I asked for individuals to express their thanks to the Lord for something very specific and to confine it to a sentence. One said, "I thank God for my wife." Another thanked God for salvation.

As each sentence was spoken, I reached out my hand as though I were picking a flower, and then I placed that flower into the bouquet I was collecting in my left hand. After many persons had offered thanks to God, I asked everyone to stand while I presented the bouquet to the Lord. It seemed that I had hardly begun to offer their thanks to God when we became very conscious of the presence of God. Thanksgiving moved into praise, and our praise lifted us into worship. A session that had been dull became lively, and from that point on the teaching of the Word produced almost immediate response from the people. We had found our way into God's presence through thanksgiving.

This, of course, is no new revelation. As far back as Solomon's day, this principle worked. At the dedication of the magnificent temple that David had conceived and Solomon had constructed...

> It came to pass, when the trumpeters and singers were as one, to make one sound to be heard in praising and thanking the Lord, and when they lifted up their voice with the trumpets and cymbals and instruments of music, and praised the Lord saying: "For He is good, for His mercy endures forever," that the house, the house of the Lord, was filled with a cloud, so that the priests could not continue ministering because of the cloud; for the glory of the Lord filled the house of God (2 Chronicles 5:13,14).

God's manifested presence, in the form of a cloud of glory, came into the temple when the musicians began to give thanks to the Lord and to praise God in unison. Perhaps to become aware of God's presence we need to unite our hearts in thanking God. We need not create a route into God. That avenue has already been constructed, and its name is Thanksgiving. It is a wide street, and there is seldom a congestion of traffic on it.

It may well have been before the days of Solomon that a psalmist, inspired of the Holy Spirit, wrote, "Oh come, let us sing to the Lord! Let

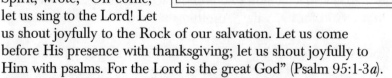

Until thanksgiving is expressed, it is merely a thought.

us shout joyfully to the Rock of our salvation. Let us come before His presence with thanksgiving; let us shout joyfully to Him with psalms. For the Lord is the great God" (Psalm 95:1-3a). Singing, joyful shouting, and the giving of thanks are all interrelated. The thanks is the motivation, while the shout is the expression. The song releases the emotion of a thankful heart.

It is possible to get emotional in responding to God without actually expressing thanks to Him. It is also possible to be "thinkful" without becoming thankful. Thanksgiving means the giving of thanks. Until it is expressed, it is merely a thought. Although God can read the secret thoughts of our hearts, we need to know those thoughts and make them gel; we need to express them with words for our own sake as well as for the sake of others. How many times has a burdened brother been lifted into God's presence just by hearing another express thanks? If one of the guests seated at the dinner table turns to the hostess and says, "Thank you for a most delicious meal," it is natural for all the other guests to join in with "Yes, thanks." Similarly, when one saint gives vocal thanks to God in the presence of other believers, many are likely to be prodded to express their personal thanks to God.

When we "come with thanksgiving," we can expect to arrive in God's presence, but it is unlikely that we will arrive alone. There is sweet fellowship in the offering of thanks. Just as there is a contagion of expressed thanks, there is also a camaraderie in thanksgiving. A common thanks offered to a specific person knits the "thankers" together as a unit. This is seen at a ball game. When many thousands of individuals unite in shouting for the home team, they form an invisible bond that links their hearts as one. Public praise and thanks offered to God work the same way. At conventions I have noticed that persons from different churches and religious heritages often have acted as bystanders and observers of what was being presented from the platform—that is, until they got involved in praising and thanking the Lord. Then they seemed to melt into one responsive person. Differences were ignored, strangeness dissipated, and a bond of fellowship was formed.

This giving of thanks in public should never replace the expression of thanks in our personal prayer lives. Just as Israel was encouraged to "enter into His gates with thanksgiving," so we should let the expression of our thanks bring us to the entrance of God's outer court. Our thanks can bring us from our "tents" to His tabernacle. Thanksgiving is a means of approach to God. It is a promised route into Him, and it is a most practical way to approach Him. Long before we ask for anything new, we must learn to express our honest thanks for what He has already done in us, for us, and through us.

Thanksgiving Is a Response to God's Performance

In one of the Songs of Ascents, psalms that were sung by Israelite pilgrims walking to Jerusalem to attend one of the required feasts, we read, "When the Lord brought back the captivity of Zion, we were like those who dream. Then our mouth was filled with laughter, and our tongue with singing. Then they said among the nations, 'The Lord has done great things for them.' The Lord has done great things for us, whereof we are glad" (Psalms 126:1-3). What God had already done for them was sufficient reason for singing, shouting, and giving of thanks.

How often we are like the indulged child at Christmas. The gifts presented are so numerous that one is thrown aside while another is opened. When the last gift has been opened, the child, excited at having received so much in such a short time, cries, "Is that all?" The lavish provision stirs more greed than gratitude. Perhaps maturity will change this in the child, but what about Christians who look mature but manifest more greed than gratitude? They need to take a look at the presents on the floor and enjoy what they have received rather than constantly raise an open palm to God for "more."

It is God's pleasure to give to His children, but it would greatly increase His pleasure if His people would say, "Thank You," for those gifts He has given to them. Paul told us, "All things are for your sakes, that grace, having spread through the many, may cause thanksgiving to abound to the glory of God" (2 Corinthians 4:15). Abundant grace should trigger great gratitude.

A little later in this letter, Paul spoke of God's abundant supply and our responsibility to share it with others. He wrote, "You are enriched in

> When we can see His hand behind every gift we receive, our thanksgiving will go directly to Him.

everything for all liberality, which causes thanksgiving through us to God. For the administration of this service [liberality] not only supplies the needs of the saints, but also is abounding through many thanksgivings to God" (2 Corinthians 9:11,12). In referring to the gift of liberality, Paul said that love offerings not only supply the finances needed, but they equally induce much thanksgiving to God. God may channel His gifts through people, but the true source of supply is God Himself. When we can see His hand behind every gift we receive, our thanksgiving will go directly to Him. Paul concluded that theme by saying, "Thanks be to God for His indescribable gift!" (2 Corinthians 9:15).

Why don't we bring thanksgiving into our prayer time? Often we simply fail to meditate upon what God has done for us. No matter how serious our present may be or how fearful the future may look, God has been faithful and gracious in our past. We may not yet be what we desire to become, but we are not now what we once were. The grace of God has been at work within us transforming our lives and sustaining us in our daily walk.

When my wife and I seemed unable to sell our house in Atlanta and feared we might lose the house we had purchased in Phoenix, we sat down to review our desperate need. Having discussed the many ramifications of our situation, I felt impressed to say, "But God has done so much for us in this move already."

My wife joined me in recounting the various interventions He had made in helping us obey His voice in moving to this new location. Before long we were so overjoyed with what God had done for us that instead of continuing to plead with Him to intervene, we thanked Him for the intervention we had already experienced. Joy replaced sorrow, and faith dominated our fears. Our present situation remained unchanged, but our relationship to God was transformed by the single act of offering thanks to Him.

In the final book of the Bible, we are allowed to see that "all the angels stood around the throne and the elders and the four living creatures, and fell on their faces before the throne and worshipped God, saying: 'Amen! Blessing and glory and wisdom, thanksgiving and honor and power and might, be to our God forever and ever. Amen'" (Revelation 7:11,12). The offering of thanks is neither confined to earth nor is it limited to the dimension of time. All eternity will echo

> All eternity will echo with the expression of thanks to God by the redeemed and the heavenly creatures who need no redemption.

with the expression of thanks to God by the redeemed and the heavenly creatures who need no redemption. God is worthy of all thanks, and He is deserving of thanksgiving by all. Here on earth, our thanksgiving is limited and tainted by our humanity, but the day is coming when we shall stand with these mighty ones and thank God in ways and with emotions we have never before been able to explore.

Thanksgiving Refocuses Our Perspective

Because we have never been able to think and respond at levels higher than our present experience, we can only guess what it will be like to thank God while standing in His glorious presence around His eternal throne. In his beautiful chapter on love, Paul admitted, "For we know in part and we prophesy in part. But when that which is perfect has come, then that which is in part will be done away.... For now we see in a mirror, dimly, but then face to face. Now I know in part, but then I shall know just as I am known" (1 Corinthians 13:9,10,12). Because we are seeing in a mirror that is losing its silver backing, we get a distorted and partial picture of what God has done and what He is doing, and this limits greatly the level of our thanksgiving to Him. Limited vision of God always distorts our responses to Him.

If we could see as God sees, we would recognize that He views all that we have done through His forgiveness. God observes us through the cross of Jesus. We would also learn that He sees what He has done through the filter of His grace. None of it was earned or deserved. All of it was made available through His grace. If we could see with divine vision, even for a moment, we would know that God views what He has provided for us through glasses colored "Christ Jesus." He sees nothing from our perspective; He sees all things through the cross, through His grace and through Jesus Christ. This, in itself, should induce great thanksgiving in the church on earth.

Because we see "in a mirror dimly," we see things not only distorted and partial; we also see things in reverse or mirror image. The nearest object is what generally catches our view, and our own self-image is usually the nearest image. Anyone who looks consistently at his or her image will lose fervent thanksgiving to God. Either we will be overwhelmed with our failures and blemishes, or we will be overwhelmed with our successes and fall into pride.

Paul told Timothy, "I thank Christ Jesus our Lord who has enabled me, because He counted me faithful, putting me into the ministry, although I was formerly a blasphemer, a persecutor, and an insolent man" (1 Timothy 1:12,13a). The negative self-image caused Paul to look away from himself to the Lord Jesus who had called him and changed him from a persecutor to a preacher of the gospel. This simple act of thanksgiving restructured Paul's perspective about himself.

During a time of overwork and stress, I became depressed, though I did not recognize it as such. When my sister, Iverna Tompkins, came to church where I

> I was driving myself harder and harder without coming to grips with my real feelings.

was headquartered, she sat me down and said, "Judson, do you realize that you have the classic symptoms of depression?" I was driving myself harder and harder without coming to grips with my real feelings, although I could admit that my self-image was at a very low level. In the mercy of God, during the next few weeks, I received an unusually large number of letters and phone calls expressing thanks for the books I had written. Years before I had learned to take all public approval to God, to hand it to Him as a bouquet of thanksgiving. That's what I did at this time and it jump-started my giving of thanks to the Lord. As I kept my eyes off myself and focused them upon Him, my depression waned, and I stepped back into a confident walk with Him. I needed to get my eyes off myself and focus them upon God.

An even more classic example of this is to be found in the Book of Jonah. Unwilling to preach God's message to Israel's enemies, Jonah tried to flee from God—only to end up spending three long days in the belly of a great fish that God had prepared. Jonah described the sensation of being in the fish: "The waters surrounded me, even to my soul; the deep closed around me; weeds were wrapped around my head. I went down to the moorings of the mountain; the earth with its bars closed behind me forever" (Jonah 2:5,6a).

Human nature being what it is, it is likely that Jonah's first "belly" thoughts were entirely self-centered. He had the world's most unusual pity party, but somewhere in this time of introspection, his attention turned to the God he had spurned and whose commission he had rejected. In spite of his circumstances, and in the midst of God's punishment for rebellion, Jonah said, " 'I will sacrifice to You with the voice of thanksgiving; I will pay what I have vowed.' ... So the Lord spoke to the fish, and it vomited Jonah onto dry land" (Jonah 2:9,10).

Jonah's thanks to God (rather than incrimination) brought him out of the fish and gave him still another chance to fulfill the commission God had given him.

Perhaps one of the most positive by-products of giving thanks to God is that it refocuses our perspective by causing us to look to Jesus. As we give thanks, we look away from self, from success, from failure, from ambition, and from circumstances. We cannot thank God successfully while focusing our minds upon anything other than God Himself. To see Him is to love Him, and when we love Him, we will brag a lot on Him and praise Him continually. All seasons of prayer should budget time for giving thanks to the Lord, not only because He is worthy of our praise, but because we desperately need the redirecting it will bring to our lives. The person who gives God thanks shows not only an ability to express gratitude, but a willingness to involve himself or herself with Someone who is greater.

Thanksgiving Focuses on the Positive

So much of our praying is negative. We share with God all our burdens, fears, anxieties, and frustrations while consuming much time and energy giving God "unknown information." While there is value in this kind of praying in that it releases these negatives from our hearts and minds, that release will be temporary unless the negatives are replaced with positives. Pouring out our fear before the Lord should be followed by receiving His faith. Expressing information to God needs to be followed with receiving information from God. If there is not a trade-off of negatives for positives, we may well magnify and exaggerate our situation and come away from prayer in an emotional condition worse than when we started.

In the passage where Paul exhorts us to pray with thanksgiving, he added, "Finally, brethren, whatever things are true, whatever things are noble, whatever things are just, whatever things are pure, whatever things are lovely, whatever things are of good report, if there is any virtue and if there is anything praiseworthy—meditate on these things" (Philippians 4:8).

What we think finds expression in our life-style. The wise man of the Old Testament said, "For as he thinks in his heart, so is he" (Proverbs 23:7a). We may conceal our true thoughts from most of our acquaintances, but close observation will reveal our true thoughts. There is no closer relationship than in intimate prayer. It is then that the secrets of our hearts are revealed both to God and to ourselves. When a believer is communicating privately with God, all of the positive words uttered in public praying tend to be toned down; the true attitude of life is expressed in the private place. Far too often that underlying attitude is negative.

For this reason the Word exhorts us, "Be anxious for nothing, but in everything by prayer and supplication, *with thanksgiving,* let your requests be made known to God" (Philippians 4:6, italics added). Repeatedly, the Bible urges us to bring our petitions before God—even "boldly" (see Hebrews 4:16). But God's Word also teaches us to mix our petitioning with thanksgiving. One reason for this is expressed when Paul was challenging us to walk in Christ Jesus, "...established in the faith...

abounding in it with thanksgiving" (Colossians 2:7). Our situation may be adverse and our emotions may be negative, but when we approach God in His faith, we can thank Him for His promises and for making provision to bring us through, or out of, our disturbing situation.

Even though our thanksgiving will reflect our level of faith, it equally reveals our relationship with God. David said, "I will praise the name of God with a

> Often it is in our time of greatest need that we receive our greatest revelation of Him.

song, and will magnify Him with thanksgiving" (Psalm 69:30). When our praying can rise above our feelings and our problems to behold our God, the natural response of a redeemed soul is to "give thanks at the remembrance of His holy name" (Psalm 30:4b). He is unchanged no matter what our circumstances. His nature and His name are constant, and "His mercy endures forever" (see Psalm 136). Our praying must bring our thoughts higher than ourselves so that we will behold God in the midst of our troubles, for often it is in our time of greatest need that we receive our greatest revelations of Him.

One year when I was ministering in France, I was awakened in the early hours of the morning with a realization that my mother-in-law was dying. I phoned home and found this to be true. I assured my wife that I would fly home as soon as I could get a seat. As I headed back to the States, I dreaded playing the role ahead of me. I am the last surviving male member of this family, and I knew that much of the responsibility for the funeral would be on my shoulders. I would also have to undergird emotionally the three sisters and the surviving aunt.

When we all gathered in the funeral parlor to view Mom Eaton, I challenged the family to be thankful that the years of suffering were over and that Mother was at home with Jesus and reunited with her husband. In the mercy of God, a real spirit of thanksgiving gripped our hearts. Replacing the deep sorrow, it became the prevailing attitude during that week.

After the funeral, the director told me, "I wish that more Christians could display their joy in God during times of grief and sorrow. This has been a dynamic demonstration of faith in God."

Later, I received letters from unsaved members of the family expressing their gratitude at how the funeral was handled. The husband of one of my nieces phoned me long distance to say that he had sensed the reality of God for the first time in his life.

There was no hilarious rejoicing—that would have been a violation of deep sorrow—but there was a genuine thanksgiving that God does all things well. As we gave thanks, the emotions that I expected to deal with were reversed. Some even experienced a higher revelation of God than ever before. The giving of thanks changed our attitudes from introspective grief to "extrospective" thanksgiving to God which caused us to deal with our Maker rather than with our loss.

Note that in his concluding charges, Paul told the Thessalonian believers, "*Rejoice* always, *pray* without ceasing, in everything *give thanks*; for this is the will of God in Christ Jesus for you" (1 Thessalonians 5:16-18, italics added). God urges us to approach Him in a positive attitude of rejoicing and thanksgiving. This is His perfect will for our lives.

Thanksgiving Becomes Positive Petitioning

The Gospels tell us that Jesus had great compassion on the multitude that stood all day listening to Him teach. He sensed their hunger and asked the disciples to find out what food was available. The disciples could find only seven loaves and a few small fish. When these were presented to Jesus, "He commanded the multitude to sit down on the ground. And He took the seven loaves and gave thanks, broke them and gave them to His disciples to set before them.... So they ate and were filled, and they took up seven large baskets of leftover fragments" (Mark 8:6,8).

Four thousand people were satisfied by this miracle of Christ Jesus, but Jesus didn't even petition the Father to multiply the food. He thanked Him for the miracle. A similar pattern was followed in the feeding of the 5,000 on another occasion. In spite of the magnitude of the need, and the logistics of the miracle, Jesus did not plead, beg, or even petition. He merely thanked God for the miracle.

When Jesus stood at the graveside of His friend Lazarus, He said, "Father, I thank You that You have heard me." Then He cried out with a loud voice, "Lazarus, come forth!" (John 11:41*b*,43). Lazarus, who had been dead three days, came out of the tomb alive. The greatest miracles of the ministry of Jesus were performed after He gave thanks to the Father.

Jesus told the Jews, "I do nothing of Myself; but as My Father taught Me, I speak these things. And He who sent Me is with Me. The Father has not left Me alone, for I always do those things that please Him" (John 8:28*b*,29). Jesus knew the will of His Father, so He did not need to petition Him; He merely thanked Him and then got on with the business at hand.

There is a level of prayer in which God makes His promises so real to us that we believe them implicitly. As we approach the need or the obstacle, our hearts well up with thanksgiving that God—Jehovah-Jireh—has foreseen that need and has seen to everything; all we need to do is thank Him for His promise and His provision.

During this Christmas season, I enjoyed fellowshipping with my youngest daughter and her family. When I realized how little workspace she had in her kitchen, I suggested to her husband, an architect, that an "island" placed in the kitchen would nearly double her counter space. Within a few minutes, he had sketched a design, and my granddaughter's husband, a cabinet-maker, gave us a bid on its cost. I signed a blank check and handed it to my daughter telling her to order it. She threw her arms around me and said enthusiastically, "Thank you, Daddy. I had never thought of doing this, and, even if I had, we couldn't have afforded it."

She did not ask for this gift, and, after I had offered it to her,

> We do not need to re-petition for assured promises; we need but rejoice and thank God for His gracious bounty to our lives.

she did not beg me for it. She merely thanked me for the provision. Shouldn't we do similarly with God? If He said it, that settles it. We should simply believe it and thank Him for it. A promise that has been quickened to our hearts is as sure of fulfillment as money in the bank is certain to draw interest. We do not need to re-petition for assured promises; we need but rejoice and thank God for His gracious bounty to our lives.

This kind of praying does not seem to come naturally to us. We tend to think of thanksgiving only in terms of what God has already done, but the truly thankful heart can be as thankful in God's promises and provisions as in His performances. We will strengthen our faith, refocus our attitudes, and bless the Lord—if we will incorporate genuine thanksgiving into our times of prayer.

Seasons of thanksgiving will almost always lift us to a higher level of prayer. It is natural to step from thanksgiving to praising. Just as my daughter, upon receiving my promise to provide the addition to her kitchen, said, "Thank you, Daddy," and then added, "You're a wonderful daddy to me," so our thanks will spill over into praise. It is the natural response of a grateful heart.

For Reflection

1. Does it seem to you that the giving of thanks is rapidly disappearing from our American culture?
2. The Old Testament pattern of approach to God was to "enter His gates with thanksgiving." Does this work for you?
3. How can your giving thanks reverse your negative attitude?
4. Can you give God thanks even when things are not going as you desire?

rayer Ascends As the Channel for Praise

Often we don't distinguish between thanksgiving and praise because one flows naturally into the other. Perhaps the most obvious distinction is that we generally give thanks to God for what He has done, while we praise Him for who He is. Thanksgiving is concerned with performance, while praise is concerned with a person. But the Bible pictures praise as a positive response to God both for His person and for His provision. While praise is always to God, it is often coupled with exaltation for something, and at that point it shares the channel of thanksgiving.

It is the thankful heart that ascends one step higher to praise the Lord. The fearful, unbelieving, despondent, and/or deeply introspective person rarely rises to praise; for praises to flow from our spirits to our God, God must be the focus of our attention. When the psalmist told us to "enter into His gates with thanksgiving," he added, "and into His courts with praise. Be thankful to Him, and bless His name" (Psalm 100:4). Twice in this one verse, thanksgiving and praise are coupled together, and on both occasions thanksgiving is listed first. Thanksgiving seems to be the channel that leads us from our natural self-centeredness to a God-consciousness. When we thank the Lord, we actually prepare our hearts to praise Him.

In what was probably his last public act, David gathered the leaders of Israel together and challenged them to present lavish gifts to God for the construction of the temple that his son Solomon would build. When their offerings were placed alongside his lavish gifts, "David blessed the Lord before all the assembly; and David said: 'Now therefore, our God, we thank You and praise Your glorious name'" (1 Chronicles 29:10,13). David blessed, thanked, and praised the Lord in one brief statement, and so may we. God is so great and so worthy of our praise that we dare not be limited to a single method of response to Him. Nor should we try so hard to distinguish between the ways of responding to God that we enter into empty ritual. We simply want to release deep appreciation and attitudes of reverence.

While all of this is true, it seems obvious that praise is a higher expression to God than thanksgiving, because praise most often centers on His person. Praise flows out of a vertical concept and is released in a vertical expression.

Perhaps the most-used method to express praise is song. It is especially valuable for congregational worship, for it unites us to a single theme, supplies us with a ready-made vocabulary, and gives us a dynamic rhythm of expression that can stir our emotions to join in our praising.

The best praise sessions incorporate diversity and make room for a variety of ways to release praise unto God. What is especially meaningful to one person may not be at all meaningful to another, and what was a beautiful channel of expression in one service may not be a workable channel for the next gathering. Even a casual glance at the diversity in people who come to a service convinces me that God is, indeed, a God of infinite variety. I suspect that He especially enjoys some variation in our responses to Himself. Challenging ourselves to find different ways to express our praise to God will help prevent praise from slipping into an empty ritual.

Whether our praise is expressed with body language, a release of emotion, words of appreciation, or songs of devotion, true praise comes from deep within the spirit of a believer; his or her whole nature joins in the praise response. Very recently, Bruce Ballinger, composer of the worship chorus "We Have Come Into His House," joined with me as a worship leader during a special meeting with pastors. He sang another of his choruses that, although it was released in 1983, was new to me. It so gripped my heart that I sang it daily for a week or more. It expressed beautifully both my concepts and my feelings about praise. The words are: "My whole being praises You, Lord. My whole being praises You, Lord. And as a visible expression I lift my hands to You, but my whole being praises You, Lord."[1] Any form of praise is valid if our whole being joins in praising the Lord.

In the past fifteen years, much has been written and taught on the subject of praise. The church, at least in the United States, has taken giant strides in implementing a praise response to God as part of the public services; but we should never forget that praise is a very private matter. It is the response of one individual to his or her concept of God. Even public praise is a group of individuals blessing God at the same time and in the same place. All individual prayer time should include a great deal of praise, as it is such a positive way to contact and commune with God.

In a public service, our praise is helped along—inspired by the response of other believers, the musicians, and the worship leader. In the privacy of our personal, solitary prayer, we have to provide our own impetus to praise. Praise might not be as easy for us, yet we seldom need to go beyond our own experiences or knowledge of God's Word to find inspiration to rejoice in the Lord. Even when we are in the midst of pressure or problems, there is ample reason for us to praise God. Let me list a few reasons for praise.

Praising God for His Wonders

The sight of a sunrise or sunset should prompt our hearts to praise the Lord. When I visited the Grand Canyon, I almost involuntarily broke forth in a song of praise to God. What magnificence! What splendor! He who was responsible for such beauty was more than worthy to be praised. King David, the great praiser of the Old Testament, never lost his sense of awe when he viewed God's glorious creation. Having spent long nights gazing at the stars while tending his father's sheep, he developed a soliloquy which became part of one of his psalms. He wrote, "The heavens declare the glory of God; and the firmament shows His handiwork. Day unto day utters speech, and night unto night reveals knowledge. There is no speech nor language where their voice is not heard. Their line has gone out through all the earth, and their words to the end of the world" (Psalm 19:1-4).

It is not simply the beauty and wonder of creation that

135

causes praise to rise up within us. God's creation is a revelation of Himself. Paul wrote, "For since the creation of the world His invisible attributes are clearly seen, being understood by the things that are made, even His eternal power and Godhead, so that they are without excuse, because, although they knew God, they did not glorify Him as God" (Romans 1:20,21*a*). The visible existence of this world is declared to be proof of the invisible existence of God. Paul declared that all humanity is without excuse for not glorifying—praising—God the Creator.

This is not a biased, personal opinion. The Bible describes a view of heaven: four living creatures giving glory and

God is seen in things both big and small.

honor and thanks to God on the throne, and elders prostrating themselves crying: "You are worthy, O Lord, to receive glory and honor and power; for You created all things, and by Your will they exist and were created" (Revelation 4:11). They declare that God is worthy to be praised because of His creative ability which displays His nature. If the highest of heaven's inhabitants are moved to praise God because of creation, should not such lowly creatures as you and I rise to sing praise to God when we view His creation?

Praising God for His Works

Praising God for His creation is a beginning level for praise, but when we consider what God has done for us, our praise reaches a higher level of expression. The psalmist expressed it: "When the Lord brought back the captivity of Zion, we were like those who dream. Then our mouth was filled with laughter, and our tongue with singing. Then they said among the nations, 'The Lord has done great things for them.' The Lord has done great things for us, whereof we are glad" (Psalm 126:1-3). Joy, rejoicing, and song rise quite naturally in the heart of one who will take time to consider what the Lord has done.

We should never look back to the pit of sin from which we were delivered with any sense of longing to return. But we do ourselves a great favor if we look back occasionally to see how far the Lord has brought us in a short time. We may not yet be what we want to become, but, praise the Lord, we are not what we once were. His grace has brought us a long, long way. We "are being transformed into the same image from glory to glory, just as by the Spirit of the Lord" (2 Corinthians 3:18*b*), The prophet compared this retrospective praise to drawing water from the deep wells in a barren land:

"O Lord, I will praise You... Your anger is turned away, and You comfort me. Behold, God is my salvation, I will trust and not be afraid; for YAH, the Lord, is my strength and my song; He also has become my salvation." Therefore with joy you will draw water from the wells of salvation. And in that day you will say: "Praise the Lord, call upon His name; declare His deeds among the peoples, make mention that His name is exalted. Sing to the Lord, for He has done excellent things; this is known in all the earth. Cry out and shout, O inhabitant of Zion, for great is the Holy One of Israel in your midst!" (Isaiah 12:1-6).

It is often frustrating to walk with persons through troubled waters. There seem to be no answers to give and no solutions in sight. I have discovered, however, that if I can get these persons to look backward and recall some of the good things God has done for them, their thoughts turn from themselves and the present pressure to God and His constancy. Often their melancholy is replaced with rejoicing. No pressing problem can prevent praise when we look at God's performance in our lives.

David declared this when he wrote the following:

"I will extol You, my God, O King; and I will bless Your name forever and ever. Every day I will bless You, and I will praise Your name forever and ever. Great is the Lord, and greatly to be praised; and His greatness is unsearchable. One generation shall praise Your works to another, and shall declare Your mighty acts" (Psalm 145:1-4).

All prayer times need to include reminiscence. While proclaiming the needs of the present and our fears of the future, we should also review the past and praise God for the

137

great things He has done.
When we realize that God
lives in eternity, rather
than in time, we become
aware that our changeless
God is today what He was
yesterday. "Jesus Christ is
the same yesterday, today, and forever" (Hebrews 13:8).

> Remembering past moments with God can create intense longings for Him in the present.

Reviewing the past dealings of God restores our courage, renews our faith, and rekindles a longing for His presence.. Just as looking at a photo album can produce a longing to return to a time or place, remembering past moments with God can create intense longings for Him in the present.

Admittedly, however, present problems can so cloud our memories that we cannot recall any good thing that God has done for us. This is when we need to look at others and rejoice vicariously in what God has done for them. In times of pressure, when my spirit was so overwhelmed that I couldn't seem to find the presence of God during prayer, I have opened my Bible to the Book of Psalms and have paced the floor reading aloud while identifying with the psalm by saying, "Amen!" Invariably, I found myself praising the Lord and enjoying His presence in a very short time. This is one of the reasons that the Bible records so much of what God has done for and in persons. We can benefit from their relationships with Him.

Praising God for His Word

In all our times of devotion we must incorporate God's Word, whether reading it, quoting it, singing it, or just meditating on it. What God has said becomes the basis of what we say back to Him, and it is often our motivation for speaking to Him in the first place. Petition that is not based upon a promise flows out of desire rather than faith. But if God has said something to us, we can depend upon it as surely as we can expect a sunrise tomorrow morning. When we talk to God about this promise, it is with thanksgiving and praise.

The person whose prayer ministry has matured to the level of praise does not merely seek the promise of God's Word. He or she rejoices in everything that God has said. Worshippers find God's Word instructive, inspirational, informative, and invaluable. The wonders of God's creation tell us that there is, indeed, a God, but it is the Word of God that tells us what He is like. The Word informs us that He is available to us in our day-to-day living. The stars above and the ocean beneath cannot communicate this message.

Persons who hunger for greater depth in their prayer lives do themselves a great service by becoming familiar with Psalm 119. This chapter is unique, not only because it is the longest chapter in the Bible, but because it mentions God's Word in every one of its 176 verses. It is an acrostic of the Hebrew alphabet that extols the Word and exhorts believers to love that Word, to live in it, and to lift their voices in praise of it. "My hands also I will lift up to Your commandments, which I love, and I will meditate on Your statutes," the writer declares (v. 48).

This psalm reminds us that God's Word is a basis for our trust (v. 42), a source of our life (v. 50), a foundation for our hope (v. 147) and a lamp to our feet (v. 105). It says, "The entirety of Your word is truth, and every one of Your righteous judgments endures forever" (v. 160). The psalmist's love of and consistent embracing of God's Word induced great peace, for he wrote, "Great peace have those who love Your law, and nothing causes them to stumble" (v. 165). He further testified that God's Word infused him with rejoicing, "I rejoice at Your word as one who finds great treasure" (v. 162), and inspired great praise, "My lips shall utter praise, for You teach me Your statutes" (v. 171).

His experience should not be considered unique, for it is available to all who will love God's Word enough to spend time in it. There have been occasions when my speaking and writing schedule so consumed my time that I neglected reading the Bible. Slowly, I declined in strength, found my spiritual vision lessening, succumbed to inner turmoil, and forfeited my rejoicing praise. My first reaction was to rebuke the devil, but the Holy Spirit made me aware that I had merely departed from the means of grace afforded me in the Bible. When I returned to the discipline of reading the Word worshipfully, my life returned quickly to normal.

139

With the return to singing passages of Scripture, we are inspired to praise and rejoice in marvelous ways. At least a half dozen times, the Bible instructs us, "Sing to the Lord a new song" (Psalm 33:3; 96:1; 98:1; 144:9; 149:1; Isaiah 42:10), and twice we are told that in heaven the redeemed ones will sing a new song to the Lord (Revelation 5:9; 14:3). Perhaps we fulfill this command when we learn a chorus from the worship leader at our church, but isn't it possible that God is urging us to become so free in our spirits that we sing an extemporaneous song to the Lord? Take a verse of Scripture that warms your heart on a particular day and put a tune to it. It doesn't matter if the words and music blend in great fashion—as long as it releases your spirit to praise the Lord.

A few years ago, I was fighting fatigue. I actually had to lift my legs with my hands to climb the stairs to my motel room. Deeply distressed, I threw myself across my bed and said, "God, this isn't right. I'm out of balance. You never intended me to wear out. Please help me."

I slept well that night but, in the early hours of the morning, I had a dream: Someone I knew well sidled up to me in a church service and sang a new chorus to me. It was a paraphrase of 1 Corinthians 15:20. It exploded in my spirit. I awoke singing it. I sang it at breakfast and, fearing that I would soon forget it, I wrote it on my napkin. All day long that chorus rang in my spirit with a rejoicing that was greater than I had experienced in a long time. About church time, I realized that I was not tired. It proved to be the end of that season of extreme exhaustion. I had been healed with singing a "new song" that the Spirit had given to me. I have never invited a congregation to learn this song, for I doubt that it was given to me for others. It was a "new song" that brought my Lord and me into such intimate relationship that His presence could affect my physical body and restore me to strength. God's Word, however we may choose to appropriate it, is a real key to victorious praying. We could never praise God too much for what He has said to us.

Praising God for What He Gives

Any suggestion that we praise God for what He gives to us usually starts our memory circuits searching for records of divine healing, intervention, or provision in time of need. This is, of course, right and proper, but there is a higher way to look at what God has given to us. God has made provision for the human race that transcends any physical or emotional miracle we may have experienced individually. There are at least four major gifts that God has given to this world that form the foundation for every other thing He ever does in human experience. I refer to His gift of life, His gift of love, His gift of forgiveness, and the gift of Himself.

Unless God chooses to explain it to us in eternity, we will never understand fully either the nature or the full effects of sin. The great New Testament theologian, Paul the apostle said, "And you He made alive, who were dead in trespasses and sins" (Ephesians 2:1). We had not failed to appreciate life, nor had we fainted in the midst of life. We were dead, for sin had murdered us. We had no ability to respond to God. We responded only to the lusts of our flesh, the desires of the mind and the prince of the power of the air. We were children of wrath. (See Ephesians 2:2,3.)

In the midst of this living death, "God, who is rich in mercy, because of His great love with which He loved us, even when we were dead in trespasses, made us alive together with Christ (by grace you have been saved), and raised us up together, and made us sit together in heavenly places in Christ Jesus" (Ephesians 2:4-6).

We are not only made alive with Christ, as Paul puts it, but, as John told us, we are made alive by Christ Jesus. "This is the testimony: that God has given us eternal life and this life is in His Son. He who has the Son has life; he who does not have the Son of God does not have life" (1 John 5:11,12). This life is not attributed to us. It indwells us. At conversion, Christ comes to "dwell in your hearts through faith" (Ephesians 3:17).

This gift of life is a gift of being. We who were dead are made alive. Nothing else that God does would matter to us if we did not have spiritual existence. God brought us out of death into His eternal life. Both the natural life which we received through gestation and birth and the spiritual life which we received through redemption in Christ are gifts of God, for which we should praise the Lord.

This breath of life is an expression of God's gift of love. The

Ephesian passage that assures us of God's indwelling life tells us that it was all an expression of His love: "God...because of His great love with which He loved us...made us alive..." (Ephesians 2:4,5). In the Roman letter, Paul declared, "But God demonstrates His own love toward us, in that while we were still sinners, Christ died for us" (Romans 5:8).

We have not been born into a spiritual world only to be resented and rejected. We are wanted children. We were loved before we came into spiritual being, and we are deeply loved now that God's life is at work within us. One of the special ministries of Christ Jesus is to make us aware of God's love. Paul prayed, "That Christ may dwell in your hearts through faith; that you, being rooted and grounded in love, may be able to comprehend with all the saints what is the width and length and depth and height—to know the love of Christ which passes knowledge; that you may be filled with all the fullness of God" (Ephesians 3:17-19).

Because His love works constantly in our favor, God has given us the further gift of forgiveness. Not one of us is able to live sinlessly in divine love. John, the great apostle of love, wrote, "If we say that we have no sin, we deceive ourselves, and the truth is not in us." Then he adds, "If we confess our sins, He is faithful and just to forgive us our sins and to cleanse us from all unrighteousness" (1 John 1:8,9). What comfort! What assurance! When we violate God's love through self-centered living, forgiveness is offered.

Only the message of Christ Jesus gives persons the chance to start over. All religions of works that depend upon the observance of rules, regulations, and codes fail to offer a chance to begin anew. But God's forgiveness grants us the chance to be forgiven and to make a fresh new start in our walk with Him.

What a basis for praise! We hardly begin to approach God in our prayer when we are reminded of some impurity or some unrighteous act in our lives. The enemy uses this as a deterrent to prayer; but once we confess that sin to God and receive His forgiveness, we can rise to praise for the finished work of the cross in our lives. Every reminder of sin that has been confessed and cleansed can become a springboard for praising God for the new beginning He has extended to us.

But as wonderful as this gift of life is in giving us being, as marvelous as the gift of love is in giving us belonging, as far-reaching as the gift of forgiveness is in offering us new beginnings, nothing compares to the gift of Christ Himself that has been shared with us. How can this ever be described? John tells us that "the Word became flesh and dwelt among us, and we beheld His glory, the glory as of the only begotten of the Father, full of grace and truth" (John 1:14). Every attempt God made to bring us into His presence had failed. Mankind, with but a few exceptions, could not relate to an invisible God. So God condescended to lower Himself to our level by becoming one of us to make it easier for us to respond lovingly to Him.

The brilliant mind of Paul could not fully comprehend this gift. He wrote, "Thanks be to God for His indescribable gift!" (2 Corinthians 9:15). Indescribable? Yes! Intangible? No. John

> The matured level of that fellowship is praise unto God for this great gift of Himself which we have received.

testified, "That which was from the beginning, which we have heard, which we have seen with our eyes, which we have looked upon, and our hands have handled, concerning the Word of life...that which we have seen and heard we declare to you, that you also may have fellowship with us; and truly our fellowship is with the Father and with His Son Jesus Christ" (1 John 1:1,3).

The revelation of God in Christ Jesus came that we might have fellowship with God. The matured level of that fellowship is praise unto God for this great gift of Himself which we have received. The existence of God is attested to by His creation; the power of God is seen in His works; the ways of God can be seen in His Word. It is the gift of Himself, in the coming of Christ Jesus, that lets us clearly know just who He is. The more this revelation is impressed upon our spirits the higher and broader our praise will become, for none of us can respond to God at a level greater than our comprehension of God.

Praising God for Who He Is

Heathen religions depict their gods as harsh, cruel, sensuous beings intent only upon their own gratification. Worship of these gods is usually a placating attempt to prevent their anger from being poured out. These gods are feared, but they are not loved. They are approached with gifts, but they are not truly worshipped. They are viewed as possessing ultimate power but having a depraved nature.

Around the world, wherever the gospel has been preached, the nature of the God of the Bible has been received with relief or disbelief. People are relieved not to have to placate an angry god, but they have a difficult time believing that Jehovah God has revealed Himself as a loving, tender, concerned being who wants to have fellowship with people. The story of Christ dying on the cross to rescue us from sin just doesn't compute in their preprogrammed minds until the Holy Spirit intervenes to give them a taste of God's love.

What a cause for praise this revealed nature of our God should be to the praying individual! As we communicate with Him in prayer we can see more of His great nature than we can see in His creation. When we touch the faithfulness and lovingkindness of God, we can join David in declaring:

> I will meditate on the glorious splendor of Your majesty, and on Your wondrous works. Men shall speak of the might of Your awesome acts, and I will declare Your greatness. They shall utter the memory of Your great goodness, and shall sing of Your righteousness (Psalm 145:5-7).

We, too, must bless God's holy name both now and forever. For further study of how God has revealed His nature to us through the compound or covenant names He uses for Himself, please see my book *Worship As David Lived It*. As we learn to praise these specific names, we release God to function in our lives in a manner consistent with that particular revelation.

When we need healing, we praise Jehovah-Rapha, "The Lord Our Healer," and if we are in turmoil and confusion, we praise Jehovah-Shalom, "The Lord Our Peace." There is no human need that God, as revealed, cannot meet. We can either plead our need, or we can praise the name of God that will address our need. Even if we choose to petition God, those petitions are more likely to be answered when they are based upon God's nature than when based upon His promises. When we respond to who God is, we are always on firmer foundation than when we respond to what God has said. While we know that God will honor His Word, we also know that God cannot violate His very being. His revelation to Moses was "...I AM WHO I AM..." (Exodus 3:14). God is not who we may think He is; He is who He has revealed Himself to be, and that is far greater than anything we will ever need from Him.

As we become more and more aware of God's nature, we develop higher and higher appreciation for the gifts He has given to us, for it is as we praise Him for who He is that we enter into the benefits of who He declares Himself to be.

Like the young woman who does not understand what caused her to move from loving the attention and gifts to loving the person who was giving them, we can reach a point where we don't pay much attention to God's gifts because we have finally seen the Giver. When we realize that every gift is an expression of His love—that He loves us—we must either flee from this love or be captured by it. It cannot be safely flirted with nor treated lightly. We move from being recipients of divine favor to being involved personally with the God of love.

As we learn to praise the Lord for Himself and Himself alone, we are prepared to step to the highest level of prayer that it is possible for a mortal to enter—adoration.

For Reflection

1. Do you stop with the giving of thanks or does it lead you into praise?
2. List three things for which you could instantly praise God.
3. What part does prayer play in releasing our praise?

# *rayer Ascends As the Channel for Adoration*

The word adoration comes from the Latin word *adorare* which means: "to pray" "to entreat" or "to do homage or to worship." The Latin root is *os* (*otis*), "mouth." The word may have evolved from the Roman practice of applying the hand to the mouth as an act of respect. In its truest sense, adoration is the act of paying homage to a divine being.

The King James translators did not choose to use the word adoration, but in the Old Testament it is demonstrated in such action as putting off the shoes (Exodus 3:5), bowing the knee (Genesis 41:43) and kissing the hand (Psalm 2:12). When Job said, "If I have observed the sun when it shines, or the moon moving in brightness, so that my heart has been secretly enticed, and my mouth has kissed my hand; this also would be an iniquity deserving of judgment; for I would have denied God who is above" (Job 31:26-28), he intimated clearly that kissing the hand was considered an act of worship. Even putting the hand to the mouth implied the highest degree of reverence and submission (see Job 21:5; 29:9).

As used in our society today, adoration is an intense admiration that lifts us in reverence to worship and to the expression of that worship in various outward acts. It includes both the inward attitudes of the heart and the physical expression of those feelings. *The International Standard Bible Encyclopedia* states: "Adoration is perhaps the highest type of worship, involving the reverent and rapt contemplation of the Divine perfection and prerogatives, the acknowledgment of them in words of praise, together with the visible symbols and postures that express the adoring attitude of the creature in the presence of his Creator."

Adoration involves a person's whole being. The mind

comprehends the love and grace of God; the will sanctions what the mind understands and yearns to appropriate the revelation of God in Christ Jesus; the emotions are stirred to their maximum intensity in responding with unearthly delight, unspeakable joy, and unsurpassed peace. Adoration inspires love and devotion so intense that it surpasses our understanding. Because words alone are usually impotent when it comes to expressing such depth of response, we are often forced to express adoration with song or physical activity—spontaneous or in liturgical form.

Adoration of God always involves interaction with God. It is never an attitude or action about God; it is always unto God. It is far too personal to be a congregational action, although many persons sometimes respond in adoration to God under the same stimuli and at the same time. On other occasions, what stimulates one person to adoration will barely move another person to praise. The depth of response is not always proportional to the measure of the stimuli. Our inner appreciation, mental comprehension, and emotional freedom or repression all contribute to the measure of our response— whether it be thanksgiving, praise, or adoration. The greater our involvement with the person of God, the more elevated our response is likely to be. When concentrating on the benefits of God's blessings, we seldom rise beyond the level of praise.

Worshippers—people who engage in adoration—have learned to respond to the love of God, and they find it relatively easy to pour out their love before the Lord. As I have said so many times in my books on worship, "True worship is love responding to love." Adoration is merely a highly refined way of receiving God's love and passing it back with intense feeling and devotion. It's an exciting love relationship. The method of expression will vary from person to person and from day to day, but the excessive attachment of love remains constant. We are loved, and He has become our Beloved.

Attitudes in Adoration

All worship is the expression of our thoughts and emotions. There can be no ritual to worship, for performance alone can never be classified as worship—not even a low form of worship. Since worship is a response to a Person, we must be in His presence when we worship. We stand before Him and release the inner attitudes that flow as a result of our encounter with Him.

In my last pastorate, God helped me discover the step that leads from praise to worship. I began to be aware of a deep affection for Him that didn't even seem to be "religious." I was in love with God, and of course being in love calls forth transparency and honesty.

Finding it difficult to communicate with God candidly, I felt challenged to turn to the Book of Psalms. David seemed to know how to communicate with God. For many weeks, I spent an hour or more in the early morning hours walking up and down the center aisle of the church reading a psalm aloud to Him. After each verse, I would pause and say "amen!" if I could honestly relate to it. Sometimes it seemed that David spoke too harshly to God, and my response would be, "Lord, I didn't say that. David did." But gradually I learned to speak my emotions to Him rather than to repress them under some pious phrases that sounded spiritual.

During this season, my perception of God was greatly enlarged. David emphasized the sovereignty of God. I never had. David seemed to worship an unlimited God. I limited Him with my doubts and fears. David spent more time praising Him than petitioning Him, and almost always his petitions were followed by praise. I needed to learn this. While David never lost sight of the greatness of God, he saw Him as the special object of his love. As I joined David in singing songs of love to the Lord, I fell in love with Jesus all over again. I had entered into a new relationship with Him. Like David, my delight was in the Lord.

I thoroughly enjoyed the sensation of "being in love" with God, but I didn't know how to express my feelings without sounding romantic. Often I wept before the Lord—more as a release of my frustrations than as an act of worship. Being a person of words and having preached from the age of seven, I was unaccustomed to being tongue-tied. But I was used to dealing with facts—not feelings. I was neither in touch with

149

my feelings, nor had I learned how to communicate those feelings with words.

During this season of ardent affection for God and equally intense frustrations in trying to express those feelings, the Holy Spirit directed my attention to the Song of Solomon. Although I had read this book every time I read the Bible through, it had never spoken to me before. Now I saw Solomon as a type of the Lord and the Shulamite woman as a type of the bride of Christ, of which I am a part. The language exchanged between Solomon and the Shulamite was the language of love. Neither was concerned with theology; each was concerned with the other; and all communication was an attempt to put into words the inner thoughts and feelings that had been stirred while in the presence of the other.

I used some of this language discreetly in my private prayer times. Instead of being rebuked or censored, I found that God received these expressions of love and responded accordingly. For weeks I cried, "Let him kiss me with the kisses of his mouth—for your love is better than wine" (Song of Solomon 1:2). This prayer released some of the deep yearnings of my spirit, and it focused my mind on what I wanted—love expressed between God and myself.

Becoming comfortable with this, I was able to progress to joining the woman in saying, "Because of the fragrance of your good ointments, your name is ointment poured forth; therefore the virgins love you. Draw me away!" (Song of Solomon 1:3,4a). Having found the delight of His kisses, I realized that I wanted His name. I was ready for a lifetime commitment with God. The very mention of His name filled my life with joy—and it still does. Just as a young lover might carry a handkerchief that has been anointed with his love's perfume (he knows that every whiff of the fragrance will stir thoughts of love in his mind), so the very mention of the name of Jesus caused love to rise within me.

As I grew more and more comfortable with this, I taught the Song of Solomon to my congregation on Thursday evenings. I taught the book verse by verse for nearly three years. About the time I completed chapter five, I left that church for the traveling ministry in which I am now engaged. I have probably received more positive comments about those tapes than any Bible study I have ever recorded.

This reaction indicates to me that most of us have difficulty speaking the language of love to God. Some are embarrassed to speak affectionately to God, especially men. Others have difficulty keeping their thoughts from slipping into physical lust. After all, the language is one we usually associate with physical passion. But one set of emotions can and must serve both our physical beings and our spiritual natures. The feelings are neither good nor bad. It is the object of those feelings and how they are directed to that object that determines their value.

The Shulamite had no difficulty saying, "I am my beloved's, and his desire is toward me. Come, my beloved, let us go forth to the field; let us lodge in the villages... There I will give you my love" (Song of Solomon 7:10-12). Those who learn to rise to adoration seldom have difficulty saying this. Love longs to be put into words. As Jesus taught us, "For out of the abundance of the heart the mouth speaks. A good man out of the good treasure of his heart brings forth good things" (Matthew 12:34b-35a).

Actions in Adoration

Praise may lead to adoration, but adoration is far higher than praise. The extravagant love that is released in adoration is seen occasionally in the relationship between a husband and wife, but it is more frequently observed in the relationship between an animal and its master. I once had a large dog that would sit on the floor and stare at me with such adoration that I couldn't help but respond to his desire for my touch. Without words, without touch, even without a bark or whine, he could communicate extravagant love. It was all in his posture and in his eyes.

In our human relationships there are times when love is better communicated without words. A touch, a kiss, a smile, a gesture, or even the language of the eyes often says what words cannot say. Emotions do not need to be defined to be expressed. Quite often the entire mood of love is broken by a poor choice of words, which sometimes create detours in our thinking.

What is true in our interpersonal associations is equally true in our relationship with God. Words are important. Words to God direct our thought patterns, express our feelings, and release our emotions. They force us to crystallize our thinking and to become specific in directing those thoughts to Him. But for all of their value, words are often imperfect vehicles for transporting deep affection. There are times when they are not only inadequate; they are absolutely unnecessary. When Jesus was in the home of Lazarus, the two sisters cared lovingly for His needs. On one occasion, however, Mary's devotion to Christ was so overwhelming that she sat at His feet listening to Him talk:

> But Martha was distracted with much serving, and she approached Him and said, "Lord, do You not care that my sister has left me to serve alone? Therefore tell her to help me." And Jesus answered and said to her, "Martha, Martha, you are worried and troubled about many things. But one thing is needed, and Mary has chosen that good part, which will not be taken away from her" (Luke 10:40-42).

Martha was juggling many tasks, but Mary had zeroed in on adoring Jesus. Just sitting at His feet, listening to His words, and looking into His face fulfilled her whole nature. She expressed her adoration with quiet body language. At that moment, nothing in life was more important to her than being with Jesus. Similarly, there are times when silence helps to concentrate a believer's full attention on the Lord Jesus. Love flows softly between the saint and the Savior, and sound would seem to break the spell. The wonder of the gaze and the excitement of the heart all ascend gloriously as an act of adoration to God.

It is likely that no man of the Old Testament expressed his adoration of God more completely than David. His psalms ring with praise; poetic exaltation rises to adoration of God. He loved Him passionately, and he said so fearlessly. Whether he functioned as shepherd, soldier, musician, or king, he did everything unto his God. He sang unto God, danced before the Lord, and conquered whole nations in Jehovah's name. He ascribed greatness to the Lord, gave lavishly to Him, and served Israel in the fear of God. Yet even this active, forceful king knew that there were times when deep, ardent affection could best be expressed to God in quiet tones. He wrote, "Meditate within your heart on your bed, and be still. Selah" (Psalm 4:4). He also said, "He leads me beside the still waters" (Psalm 23:2).

In the New Testament also a complete adoration to God is described. Words, songs, fervent activities, and body language express worship, especially in the book of Revelation. There the heavenly beings worship God by prostrating themselves before Him. At times they sing, and on at least one occasion they wave palm fronds to express their love.

> The very spontaneity of adoration will require diversity of expression.

Like human love, adoration will be expressed in a variety of ways. If it is not, it becomes stale and stifled. The very spontaneity of adoration will require diversity of expression.

From Anguish to Adoration

It may seem that an eternity separates anguish and adoration, but very often they are but a step apart. The sinner who is struggling with guilt and conviction finds himself or herself in the abyss of anguish. But there a simple repentant prayer can bring instant relief, moving the mood of the soul from loathing self to loving the Savior. In an instant of time, anguish over sin is replaced with adoration of God.

The First Book of Samuel begins with the story of Hannah, who made the move from anguish to adoration. Hannah was one of the two wives of Elkanah. The other wife, Peninnah, had children, but Hannah had none; and Peninnah made Hannah miserable because of her barrenness. This was especially evident during the celebration of the annual feast of the Lord when Hannah wept bitterly in her grief (see 1 Samuel 1:7).

Although Hannah was childless, she was the special love of her husband. To show his love he even gave her double portions of the sacrifice. She would not eat them, though, and concerned Elkanah asked, "Why do you weep? Why do you not eat? And why is your heart grieved? Am I not better to you than ten sons?" (1 Samuel 1:8).

Almost any husband knows the answer to that last question. This wife yearned to be a mother! No husband, however loving, could fill that place in her heart. Hannah poured out her anguish to the Lord in an inaudible prayer. She promised the Lord that if He would give her a son, she would give that son to the service of the Lord. Eli, the priest, mistakenly accused Hannah of drunkenness; but when Hannah explained the anguish of her soul and the pledge of her heart, Eli said, "The God of Israel grant your petition which you have asked of Him" (1 Samuel 1:17).

When Samuel, the child God gave her, was old enough to survive without his mother's care, Hannah took him to the house of God at Shiloh and presented him to Eli. She wanted the child to spend the rest of his life serving God and the priests. While this act of consecration was costly, Hannah saw the fulfillment of her vow as an act of adoration to God who had removed her reproach and fulfilled the deep longings of her heart.

Eli, Samuel, and Hannah worshipped the Lord in this act of dedication (see 1 Samuel 1:28): "And Hannah prayed and said: 'My heart rejoices in the Lord; my horn is exalted in the Lord. I smile at my enemies, because I rejoice in Your salvation. There is none holy like the Lord, for there is none besides You, nor is there any rock like our God'" (1 Samuel 2:1,2).

Rather than regret her vow, Hannah rejoiced in God's great provision. In her exaltation of God, she quoted repeatedly from the Scriptures available in her day as though she were a scribe or a scholar. Her eyes were upon God the Giver not on Samuel the gift. Her boasting was in God rather than in her son. Like David who sang, "You have turned for me my mourning into dancing; You have put off my sackcloth and clothed me with gladness, to the end that my glory may sing praise to You forever" (Psalm 30:11,12), Hannah moved from anguish over her deficiency to adoration of her Lord for His sufficiency.

Adoration of God is the fruit of complete trust in Him. It is the paramount form of communication with Him. It is the

154

ultimate, the definitive level in prayer. Every other form of prayer is made available to remove barriers and to change our attitudes so that we can worship and adore the Lord our God.

In heaven, our prayer will be adoration. There will be no need for the confession of sin, nor will we need to petition God for anything. Our communication with God will be face-to-face, and there will be no need for intercession. Faith and submission will be automatic, and thanksgiving and praise will become spontaneous. The only overt expression prayer will take is adoration to God. All the expertise we may have developed in these earthly channels of prayer will be useless to us. Heaven's prayer time will be devoted exclusively to the release of extravagant love and affection to God. How wonderful this will be for those who have learned to adore God during their times of prayer here on the earth! Why wait until eternity to learn to adore God when He is available for our adoration every day—here and now?

Perhaps every prayer session we enter into should include the words of the chorus that has been so popular:

Father, I adore You; Lay my life before You. How I love You.
Jesus, I adore You; Lay my life before You. How I love You.
Spirit, I adore You; Lay my life before You. How I love You.[1]

For Reflection

1. Is adoration of God merely an attitude of our heart?
2. Do you feel embarrassed or ill at ease in vocally expressing your adoration of God?
3. Have you ever tried to use the language of David in expressing your adoration of God?
4. Do you think we will pray in heaven? If so, what type of prayer will it be?

Addendum

Paul so honestly admitted: "When I was a child, I talked like a child, I thought like a child, I reasoned like a child. When I became a man, I put childish ways behind me" (1 Corinthians 13:11, NIV). He was merely admitting that as life matures, so do our responses to life. Prayer is no exception.

The early chapters of this book are based very much on the truths I taught and practiced very early in my ministry. I earnestly involved myself and my congregation in prayers of confession, petition, communication, and intercession. They were, and are as always, very effective. This kind of praying never goes out of date.

At the time the earlier edition of this book was released, I was more deeply involved in prayers of faith, submission, and thanksgiving. It was certainly walking a step above the level prayer I practiced in my earlier days. It also got *me* more involved with the One to Whom I was praying than in the problem that had brought me to prayer.

Now the book has been re-edited and is re-released under a new title. I am in my mid- seventies, and prayer has taken on a fresh new perspective. While I have not totally forsaken earlier forms of prayer, it seems that as I approach the Lord in prayer, all that really matters is praise and adoration. As I have matured in my natural life, I have also matured in my prayer life. When I step through heaven's portals, I will discover that the prayers of the saints in the presence of Jesus are prayers of praise and adoration. I'm getting in practice before my arrival. I invite you to join me in that upward journey.

Love in Jesus,
Judson

Notes

Chapter 9
1. Bruce Ballenger, *My Whole Being Praises You, Lord*, 1983.

Chapter 10
1. Terrye Coelho, *Father, I Adore You*, 1972.

About the Author

Judson Cornwall has often been introduced as "the teacher we can understand," for he specializes in making God's Word applicable to everyday living.

He pastored churches on the West Coast for thirty years, spent three years as a Bible school instructor in the state of Washington, and has traveled the world as a conference speaker and teacher for over twenty-five years. He has been on the faculty of Bible schools in Selah, Washington; Plano, Texas; Brentwood, England; and Elmira, New York.

Although Dr. Cornwall seeks to maintain a balance in his teaching, his emphasis is very often on response to God through prayer, praise, and worship. He has written fifty-two books and several booklets on these topics and others. Over thirty foreign translations are currently available. (On the next page you will find a listing of books currently available.)

He is "the husband of one wife" who sometimes travels with him, and is the father of three daughters, grandfather of nine children, and great-grandfather of ten.

Dr. Cornwall serves on the advisory board of ten religious corporations and sits on the board of directors of Bridge-Logos Publishers. He is an elder at Scottsdale Worship Center in Arizona.

Books Currently Available by Judson Cornwall

These titles may be purchased at your local Christian bookstore or by placing an order through Kingdom Publishing at (800) 597-1123:

1. Let Us Praise
2. Let Us Draw Near
3. Let Us Abide
4. Let Us Enjoy Forgiveness
5. Let Us Be Holy
6. Profiles of a Leader
7. Let Us See Jesus
8. Let Us Worship
9. Elements of Worship
10. Incense & Insurrection
11. Meeting God
12. Leaders: Eat What You Serve
13. David Worshiped a Living God
14. Worship As David Lived It
15. Praying the Scriptures
16. Things We Adore
17. The Best of Judson Cornwall
18. David Worshiped with a Fervent Faith
19. Lord, It's Me Again
20. Jesus: A Living Example of Worship
21. My Father and I (Christian fathers)
22. Exhaustive Dictionary of Bible Names (with Dr. Stelman Smith)
23. It's God's War
24. The Philosophy of Worship
25. Please Accept Me (with Thomas Cornwall)
26. Five Foundations for Marriage (with Dr. Robert Cornwall)
27. The Pearlmaker (with Rev. James Cornwall)
28. On the Ash Heap with No Answers (with Dr. Iverna Tompkins)
29. The Cross: The Believer's Authority Over the Demonic (with Rev. Glenn Foster)

The following books may be ordered through Judson Cornwall's ministry by calling (602) 996-4916 or mailing an inquiry to this address:

Judson Cornwall
4335 E. Shangri-La Road
Phoenix, AZ 85028

30. Heaven
31. Let God Arise
32. What Is There About No You Do Not Understand
33. The 365-Day "Let Us" Diet (devotional)
34. Samson: Charisma Without Character
35. Jesus Is Better Than...
36. Maintaining the Miracle
37. Mrs. Judson Cornwall
38. The Sprinkled Blood
39. Back to Basics
40. Whose Love Is It, Anyway? (with Bishop Mike Reid)
41. Whose Mind Is It, Anyway? (with Bishop Mike Reid)

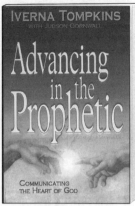

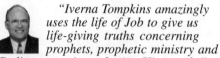

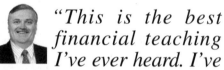

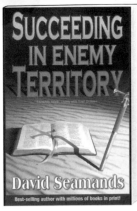

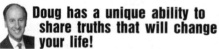
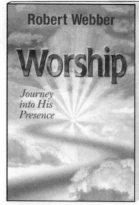

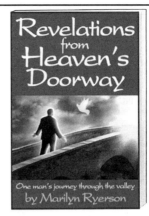

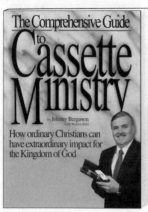

Discover how ordinary Christians can multiply the effectiveness of their whole church!

"This book was so good I could hardly put it down. This book showed me how to do everything... plus it's an abundant source of ideas. I thank God for putting this book in my hands. And I truly believe cassette ministry is a God given tool..."
– Carol Faust, Florida

As you catch the vision for cassette ministry, you'll quickly discover how to help make your entire church more effective through cassette ministry.

That's right. Anyone, anywhere can help make their ENTIRE church more effective through cassette ministry. You won't find another book like this anywhere!

The Comprehensive Guide to Cassette Ministry is loaded with practical ideas that will help you increase the effectiveness of nearly every ministry in your church. You'll discover four compelling Biblical reasons to do cassette ministry, the right – and wrong – ways to do it; how to fund your tape ministry; how to increase evangelism, teaching, and pastoral care through cassettes. You'll learn everything you could possibly want to know.

This book is helping ordinary Christians everywhere help make their entire church more effective!

The Comprehensive Guide to Cassette Ministry by Johnny Berguson

ISBN: 1-883906-12 **Only $19.97**

Code # Fire105

Get the only Bible on Cassette that you can copy and give away

Suddenly you can give copies of the New Testament on Cassette to friends. Make a copy for your school. Copy several for your outreach ministry.

Or copy it for any ministry reason you want and give it away – you won't pay one cent in royalty fees! (We just ask that you don't copy the tapes for resale or profit.) Never before has anyone, anywhere made the Bible on cassette so easily available to so many.

Two years of planning was put into this Bible on Cassette before any production started.

Unique features of The Classic℠ King James Version

- The only Bible on Cassette you can copy and give away!
- 16 Free Access℠ studio quality master cassettes of the New Testament
- Recorded at the perfect speed for comprehension and enjoyment (It's not jam-packed onto 12 cassettes to save money)
- Digitally recorded to prevent listener fatigue
- Features the phenomenal voice of Dr. Vernon Lapps

16 Master Cassettes of the New Testament

The Classic℠ King James Version Bible on Cassette
narrated by Dr. Vernon Lapps

ISBN: 1-883906-14-8 **Only $47.00**

Code # Fire105

Available at your local Christian bookstore or call toll free (800) 597-1123

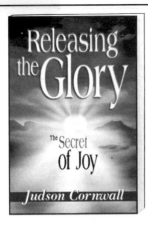
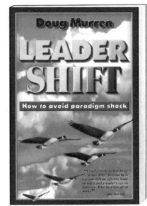

Discover the keys to effective prayer and intercession!

Intercessors, prayer warriors, and praying Christians everywhere are discovering prayer in a fresh, powerful way. *Prayer Audio Magazine™* will catapult your prayer and intercession to new levels.

God desires to communicate intimately with you through prayer. Through *Prayer Audio Magazine* you can invite the world's leading authorities into your own home to help you pray with greater effectiveness.

Each audio cassette has been prayerfully developed to help you maximize your prayer life.

Be more effective. Be informed. Pray with greater fervency and power! Get the best of *Prayer Audio Magazine* today!

The best of Prayer Audio Magazine:

- 12 audio cassettes featuring the world's leading authorities on prayer and intercession – these are 12 of the best issues ever of *Prayer Audio Magazine*
- 12 helpful listening guides (one for each cassette)
- Deluxe storage binder stores all 12 cassettes and listening guides
- Exclusive interviews and more
- Noted speakers include: Judson Cornwall, C. Peter Wagner, and Eddie & Alice Smith

"Prayer Audio Magazine *challenges us to keep pressing in to God. It keeps us informed, and brings us together to bond in prayer...*"
– Pastor Jim Ottman, Maine

Only ~~$97~~ $87 with coupon or special code on coupon **+ $9.97 shipping**
60-Day Money Back Guarantee

Call toll free (800) 597-1123

Actually experience the most powerful moves of God on the earth today
through *Renewal Audio Magazine*™!

> ### "Renewal Audio Magazine *will keep you at the front row of what God is doing and saying in the earth today.*"
> — Bob Sorge, Author of *The Fire of Delayed Answers* (and many other books)

Advance to the forefront of what God is doing throughout the earth today with *Renewal Audio Magazine*.

You can experience what God is doing in your own living room, heart, and life. *Renewal Audio Magazine* harnesses the unique power of the cassette to take you where God is moving today. You'll feel God's heartbeat with an immediacy that will excite you.

Each cassette contains critical messages from some of the most anointed men and women on earth. These men and women have been specially anointed for this hour. You'll also hear exclusive interviews and much more. You'll find your spiritual life moving to new levels with each cassette! *Renewal Audio Magazine* will both refresh and inspire you!

The best of Renewal Audio Magazine:

- 12 of the best audio cassette issues ever of *Renewal Audio Magazine* – hear from some of the most anointed men and women of our generation
- 12 listening guides (one for each tape)
- Deluxe storage binder stores all cassettes and listening guides
- Exclusive interviews and more
- Noted speakers include Francis Frangipane, Bob Mumford, Mike Bickle, C. Peter Wagner, Iverna Tompkins, and Ed Silvoso

Only ~~$97~~ **$87** with coupon or special code on coupon + $9.97 shipping

60-Day Money Back Guarantee

Call toll free (800) 597-1123